CRITIC'S CHOICE

Random House, New York

Critic's Choice

A comedy by IRA LEVIN

To

GABRIELLE

CRITIC'S CHOICE *was presented by Otto Preminger at the Ethel Barrymore Theatre, New York City, December 14, 1960, with the following cast:*

(IN ORDER OF APPEARANCE)

PARKER BALLANTINE	Henry Fonda
ANGELA BALLANTINE	Georgann Johnson
JOHN BALLANTINE	Eddie Hodges
DION KAPAKOS	Murray Hamilton
ESSIE	Billie Allen
CHARLOTTE ORR	Mildred Natwick
IVY LONDON	Virginia Gilmore

Directed by Otto Preminger

Production Designed by George Jenkins

Clothes by Oleg Cassini

The action takes place in the Ballantine apartment, near Washington Square. The time is last season. There are three acts.

"I sometimes have visions of a gag conference in which that slick character who is traditionally known as Manny bounces in, eyes ablaze, and bubbles over with: 'Listen. This guy's a dramatic critic, see? So his wife writes a play. He's *got* to review the play. Take it from there.'"

—WALTER KERR
"How Not to Write a Play"

SETTING

The Ballantines—Parker, Angela, and John—are a healthy, happy, comfortable family, and their apartment looks it. It's a duplex near Washington Square, in an elegant old house that will probably be torn down any day to make way for an NYU College of Dentistry, and more's the pity. What we see onstage is the living room, with the entrance foyer upstage center, and the door to the kitchen at stage left; the staircase, upstage right center, leading up to Parker and Angela's bedroom door, and a hallway going off right (to John's bedroom and the guest room); and downstage right a portion of Parker's study, which is something like the inside of a filing cabinet. The dining area is downstage left; a round table near a tall, sheerly draped window.

The furniture in the apartment is mostly antique; good pieces picked up at auction and tossed together with a casual disregard for period and style; a couch, the usual chairs and tables, liquor cabinet near door to study. A TV set is someplace, and so is the hand loom on which Angela started weaving a scatter rug last summer. Desk, typewriter, and many, many books in the study, some of the latter beginning to leak out and absorb the living room, like the blob in a horror movie. Lots of pictures are sprinkled around the living room walls; some of them sketches by Matisse and Dufy, some of them enlarged snapshots of various people and places. A telephone is near the couch. The entrance door and a closet are in the foyer.

The total effect is pleasant, busy, interesting, and comfortable.

ACT ONE

ACT ONE

At rise, the BALLANTINES *are discovered at breakfast, all three reading sections of the morning paper. They read in silence for a moment.*

PARKER, *sitting at center, is in his late thirties or early forties. He is wearing gray flannels, a white shirt open at the collar, and a very old and favorite cardigan.*

ANGELA, *in sweater and skirt, is sitting at* PARKER'S *right. She is twenty-seven or twenty-eight; a bright and delectable blonde.*

JOHN, *sitting opposite* ANGELA *and at* PARKER'S *left, is twelve. He is wearing slacks and a flannel shirt and isn't eating his cereal.*

PARKER *(An item from the paper)* Here's a fellow swimming the English Channel, and he's got himself all greased up— you know—and he gets cramps, and he's so slippery, they can't pull him into the boat . . .

    (ANGELA *and* JOHN *smile;* JOHN *goes back to his paper)*

ANGELA Come on now, John, just eat *some* of your cereal. Don't you want to have *energy?*

JOHN What do I need energy on Saturday for?

ANGELA *(To* PARKER*)* Explain to him why he needs energy.

PARKER *(Pointing to* JOHN's *plate)* Eat.

3

JOHN All right, all right . . .
    (*He eats and reads.* PARKER *and* ANGELA *exchange a smile*)

PARKER You're a fine one to talk; one cup of black coffee.

ANGELA I am *five pounds overweight.*

PARKER You're a skinny, scrawny wretch and I'm not letting
    another fashion magazine inside that door. Women are *not*
    supposed to have square corners.

ANGELA I won't have *square corners.*

JOHN Boy, this is the best review you've written all season.

PARKER It was a wonderful play.

JOHN Do I get to see it, or is it another dirty one?

PARKER Well, parts of it may be a bit over your head . . .
    (*To* ANGELA) If we're lucky . . .

ANGELA Oh, take him, Parker! It's so—*warm* and *bright* . . . !

PARKER (*To* JOHN, *smiling*) Next Saturday afternoon.

JOHN Good deal. Hey, this is one of mine! This one! "As
    much fun as your first circus!" That's mine! Remember!

PARKER Are you sure? It was typed.

JOHN I type them sometimes! It was in my first big batch;
    about a dozen for the white box and twenty or thirty for

the black box. A year ago. You paid me only ten cents for this.

PARKER   You were a child. I didn't want to spoil you.

JOHN   Boy, ten cents and you build half a review around it . . .
   (*He puts aside the paper*)

ANGELA   Here's a woman named Triplet who had quadruplets.

PARKER   They make those things up, so the columns come out even.

ANGELA   No, here's a picture. (*Shows him*) Aren't they cute?

PARKER (*Smiling*)   Mmm . . .

JOHN   According to Godfrey Von Hagedorn it's all psycho-somatic, your not being able to get pregnant.

ANGELA   Oh, it is, is it?

PARKER   In thirty seconds we're going to have "Spank-the-Precocious-Children Hour."

ANGELA   No, I want to hear this. Go ahead. According to God-frey Von Hagedorn . . .

JOHN   Well, he says Dad had me with Ivy, so *he's* all right, and you have a wide pelvis so *you* ought to be all right, so the trouble must be psychosomatic.

5

PARKER Would someone mind identifying Godfrey Von Hagedorn? Just for us laymen?

JOHN Godfrey, you know. *Godfrey.* The kid from downstairs.

PARKER That *peanut* who sits here and watches Wyatt Earp with you?

JOHN Mm-hmm.

ANGELA During the commercials they talk about my pelvis.

PARKER We should be honored, Angela! Think of it; right here in our own living room; Godfrey Von Hagedorn, the famous twelve-year-old gynecologist!

JOHN Godfrey *knows* all this psychosomatic stuff. His father's an analyst. Godfrey puts a glass up against the wall and listens. He says you probably feel inferior to Ivy, because she's a glamorous actress and you're just from Random House. You're afraid that your baby won't turn out as good as hers did. Me, I mean.
    (*He eats*)

PARKER You'd better watch TV down in their apartment for a while.

JOHN We can't. I'm not allowed in.

PARKER Why not?

JOHN Oh, Dr. Von Hagedorn's writing a play, and he showed me the first act, and then he asked me my opinion of it . . .

ANGELA   Godfrey does psychoanalysis for your family and you do drama criticism for his.

JOHN   Oh, sort of . . .

PARKER   I wonder if kids ever play mumblety-peg any more.

JOHN   Play *what?*

PARKER   Never mind.
          (*A beat*)

ANGELA   You know, *I've* been toying with an idea for a play . . .

PARKER   You have?

ANGELA   Mm-hmm . . . (PARKER *and* JOHN *exchange a glance*) That comedy last week, about the boarding house; it reminded me of an uncle of mine. The family character. *He* took in roomers, odd-ball types; a broken-down juggler, an old woman who kept *pigeons* in her closet . . . I ran away from home once, when I was fifteen; Mom and Sally and Marge had gotten to be too much for me. Uncle Ben took me in, and the four days I spent in that rooming house could make a *wonderful* play; funny, and tender, and moving too, in a wistful kind of way . . .

PARKER   I think I know the sort of play you mean . . . Youth learns from old age, and vice versa.

ANGELA   Mm-hmm . . .

7

PARKER The girl goes home to Mother and her sisters, willingly, and the roomers go out one by one into the no-longer-so-terrifying world; the juggler juggling again, the old woman setting free her captive pigeons . . . (ANGELA *has turned to* PARKER, *surprised and encouraged, nodding*) The final curtain would be Uncle Ben, all alone in the gathering twilight, dusting off the old placard and propping it up in the window. "Rooms For Rent."

ANGELA Yes! Yes, sort of . . . Something like that. Do you think it would go?

PARKER In Boston tryouts alone it's already folded twelve times.
   (ANGELA *glares*)

ANGELA I suppose you think you're terribly funny.

PARKER (*Touching the cheek which she averts angrily*) I thing *you're* funny. *And* tender. And moving too, in a wistful kind of way. (*Kisses the averted cheek*) I love you.

ANGELA Well, I'm just liable to try it. It isn't new stories the theatre needs; it's new insights into the old ones! You said that yourself in one of your Sunday pieces!

PARKER Did I?

JOHN Back in September.

PARKER I was dead wrong.

ANGELA I've made up my mind. I'm going to do it.

8

PARKER And with those words, flung bravely in the face of a hostile mocking world, there began the career of Angela Ballantine, or as we know her today, Lillian Hellman. Author of *Kindly Old Uncle Ben* and twice winner of the Clare Boothe Luce Award for America's Cutest Playwright. (ANGELA *turns away angrily*) Ah, come off it, Angie. You're the most wonderful girl in the world, but you're not a writer. It's all you can do to compose a letter to your mother once a week.

JOHN Dr. Von Hagedorn's play is about this noble analyst who goes around *saving* people.

PARKER Amateur night, huh?

JOHN And how.

ANGELA (*Rises*) Are you typing today or pacing and dictating?

PARKER Pacing. I want to make a start on that *Harper's* thing.

ANGELA Then may I use the typewriter?

PARKER (*A beat*) What's mine is yours.

ANGELA Thank you.
(*She takes her dishes and exits into the kitchen. A pause*)

JOHN I don't think you handled it right.

PARKER Don't worry. (*A wave of the hand*) Nothing.

9

JOHN Will she really do it?

PARKER Oh, she'll—(ANGELA *re-enters, takes the remaining dishes, and exits again*) She'll begin it, all right; the way she began that scatter rug last summer. She won't stay with it, though. A week at the most. She has all the bulldog endurance of a snowflake.

JOHN Boy, if she *does* finish it, it's going to be like Ivy all over again. *She'll* be having tryouts in New Haven and Philadelphia, and *we'll* be here, eating those *TV dinners.*

PARKER (*Smiles at* JOHN's *depression*) Hey, you know what Angie's done?

JOHN What?

PARKER Given me an idea for that *Harper's* article ... Everybody's always encouraging amateur playwrights: "Write That Play!" "Earn Those Royalties!" Somebody ought to *dis*courage them; point out the ridiculous odds, winnow the ranks a little. *"Don't* Write That Play!" How's that for an article?

JOHN I don't know ... It sounds kind of ... precious.

PARKER (*Mock outrage*) I'll give you—!

JOHN (*Rising and going to the stairs*) Well, you asked for my opinion, didn't you? (PARKER, *smiling, rises and goes into the study.* JOHN *mutters on as he climbs the stairs*) Boy, everybody asks for an opinion, and you give it to them, and then they get sore at you ...

(JOHN *exits. In the study,* PARKER *sits at the desk and takes up a portable tape recorder. He fiddles with its switches.* ANGELA *comes out of the kitchen and crosses into the study. She finds the portable typewriter in its case*)

PARKER Dishes all done?

ANGELA It's Saturday; Essie does them. (*Resting the portable on the desk*) May I have some paper, please?

PARKER (*Opening a drawer*) What do you want: white, yellow, onionskin . . . ?

ANGELA Um . . . A little of each.

PARKER (*Collects the paper, smiling; gives it to her*) The rent on the typewriter is a kiss an hour. (ANGELA *gives him a peck*) You just bought four seconds.

ANGELA (*Puts the portable on the floor as* PARKER *draws her into his lap*) Oh, Park, why do you have to be such a damn tease? Maybe I can accomplish something . . . Uncle Ben wasn't as much of a cliché as he sounds.

PARKER (*Still teasing*) He wasn't?

ANGELA *No he wasn't.*
(*She kisses* PARKER *soundly*)

PARKER Whew. You are now the proud owner of a second-hand Underwood. (ANGELA *rises, takes the portable again*)

I wish you luck, honey. I wish you *The Glass Menagerie* and *The Time of Your Life* and *Come Back, Little Sheba.*

ANGELA Now you've gone and scared me.
(*She goes out and up the stairs, and exits right.* PARKER, *smiling after her, takes up his recorder*)

PARKER Saturday, November seventh. Notes for essay: "Don't Write That Play." Opening paragraph: (*Gets up, walks around the desk*) All over nation housewives, psychiatrists, butchers, barbers, sitting down to . . . defenseless typewriters. A million plays in progress, all beginning with the maid answering the telephone and subtly feeding information. Sample dialogue: "Good afternoon. Snodgrass residence. This is the maid. Mr. Snodgrass? He's in his office and can't be disturbed. Mrs. Snodgrass? She's at the hairdresser's, prettying herself up for the big party tonight. Junior Snodgrass? Oh, he's in jail on a narcotic rap." (JOHN *enters on the balcony and comes down the stairs*) Most beginners conk out early in the game because they try to base play on personal reminiscence. This is *not* a good idea unless you are Lucrezia Borgia or Al Capone.

JOHN Hey, Dad?

PARKER Yo?

JOHN (*Entering study*) I've got one for the white box and one for the black.

PARKER Let's hear them.

12

JOHN (*A beat*) She's in the guest room, and the typewriter's going like a machine gun.

PARKER Don't *worry!* Believe me, one week and she'll toss in the sponge. We've *had* our career woman; Angie is *not* Ivy. (*Sits in the desk chair*) Come on, let's hear.

JOHN This is the white one. It's only fifteen cents. It's for a really wonderful play. (*Reads from a slip of paper*) "The stage took wing last night, and carried a fortunate audience closer, much closer, to the stars." It's just fifteen cents . . .

PARKER All right, I'll take it . . .
(*He takes the slip of paper, reaches into his pocket for change, and pays* JOHN)

JOHN And one black one. This is a dollar.

PARKER *A dollar!* You've gone mad in that room up there.

JOHN This is for a play that's absolutely awful in every department. (*Reading from a second slip*) "The actors were wooden and rigid, and so was the script. In fact *everything* last night was wooden and rigid, with one exception, and that, unfortunately, was the scenery."
(PARKER *gives* JOHN *a dollar and seizes the slip.* JOHN *runs out, closes the door, and goes happily up the stairs, while* PARKER *gets the white and black file boxes out of the desk compartment and files the two slips. The lights fade quickly and come up again as* ANGELA, *in a smock, comes out of the kitchen, thoughtfully peeling a banana*)

13

ANGELA *(Reciting to herself as she crosses toward the stairs)* Yes, Uncle Ben, I have run away from home. They don't need me there. Mother and Sally and Marge are so efficient and well organized that—that I am just the fifth wheel. *(Stopping halfway up the stairs, counting on her fingers)* Mother, Sally, Marge ... I am the *fourth* wheel? *(Continues up. On the landing, the solution hits her)* I am the *spare tire!* *(She hurries off. The telephone rings.* PARKER *opens the study door, and takes the phone)*

PARKER Hello? *(*JOHN *enters through the front door, key in hand, carrying a briefcase and* Variety*)* Yes. Just a minute, please. *(Calling upward)* Angie!

JOHN Hi.

PARKER Hi. Go call Angie, will you?

JOHN *(Right where he is, bellowing)* ANGIE!

PARKER Thanks a lot.

ANGELA *(Off right, upstairs)* What is it?
*(*JOHN *puts the briefcase and* Variety *on the couch, and takes off his coat)*

PARKER Telephone!

ANGELA *(Off)* Who is it?

PARKER *(Into phone)* Who's calling, please? *(Aloud)* S. P. Champlain!

14

CRITIC'S CHOICE

JOHN The producer?

ANGELA (*Appearing on upstairs landing, pencil in hand, wide-eyed*) The producer?
  (*A beat*)

PARKER (*Into phone*) The producer?

ANGELA Park!
  (*She flees into the bedroom, shutting the door*)

PARKER Just a second. Here she is. (*Listens, then hangs up*)
I suppose it *could* have been S. P. Champlain the laundry-man.

JOHN Is he going to be *Angie's* producer?

PARKER Of what? Act One?

JOHN She's halfway through Act Two now.

PARKER S. P. Champlain is *not* about to concern himself with
an unfinished play by an amateur playwright. Although
. . . last season he *did* put on that musical version of *An-thony Adverse* . . . (*His hand glances the phone*) Would
it hurt you very much to find out that your father listens
on extensions?

JOHN (*Coming closer*) Heck, no! Go ahead!
  (*A beat*)

PARKER No, no . . . It would hurt *me* to *have* you find out.
  (*He ruffles* JOHN's *hair*)

JOHN (*Deeply disappointed*) Ohh . . .

PARKER We'll wait. Angie'll tell us. (*Sits on the couch, takes up* Variety) What's in *Variety?*

JOHN Ivy's doing a musical in the spring.
(*He takes his coat upstage*)

PARKER I know. She called me for advice. And ignored it, of course.

JOHN (*Hanging his coat in the closet*) I don't remember Ivy ever singing.

PARKER You're a lucky boy . . .

JOHN Say, how did he find out about Angie? S. P. Champlain.

PARKER I don't know . . . She talked about the play last week, at a party we went to.

ANGELA (*Entering from the bedroom, on the landing*) Guess what!

PARKER (*Putting aside* Variety) I give up.

JOHN S. P. Champlain is going to produce your play.

ANGELA No, don't be silly. But he wants to read it as soon as I'm done. I told him what it's about and he thinks it's a great idea!

PARKER (*Rising; singing and doing a buck and wing*)
"Hello, I'm Anthony Adverse,
 And tho' this may be a bad verse,
  I'm mighty glad that I'm he-ere!"
 Doodily, doodily . . .

ANGELA (*Icily*) Every producer makes his mistakes, and S. P. Champlain has made fewer than most.

PARKER But it's the *quality* of his mistakes, not the quantity! (ANGELA *glares*) Ah, forgive me for teasing. Congratulations, darling.

ANGELA There's nothing to congratulate me for—yet. And what's more, I know he only called because I'm your wife. But he wouldn't *still* be interested after I told him about it, would he, just because of that?

PARKER No, he wouldn't, Angie.

ANGELA Well then . . . !

PARKER (*With a grin*) Just watch out if he invites you to have lunch with him. I hear the "S. P." stands for Sneaky Pincher.
    (*He exits into the study, leaving* ANGELA *on the landing, uncertain whether or not to be angry*)

JOHN Congratulations.

ANGELA Thank you. It's premature. He isn't still working on that nasty little article, is he?

JOHN (*Sitting on couch, taking up* Variety) He's making it into a book now.

ANGELA Hmm!
(*She exits right. The light irises down to spot on* JOHN *as he sits reading*)

JOHN (*Singing softly*)
"And now we'll sing you a sad verse,
Good-bye old Anthony Adverse."
Doo-doo-doo-doo-doo-deedily-doo . . .
(*The spot fades on* JOHN *and comes up on* PARKER *at the desk in the study, dictating*)

PARKER Tuesday, January nineteenth. Notes for book: "Don't Write That Play"; Chapter Twelve. Recapitulation of difficulties. Each scene tougher to write than scene before, demanding greater craftsmanship, stronger discipline, and larger waste basket. (ANGELA *enters and comes down the stairs, reverently bearing a thick manuscript. She is nervous, but her cheeks are glowing with a serene pride—rather like a new mother*) If a third act were no harder to write than a first act, the fees of the copyright office would support the entire government. The number of unfinished plays is in direct proportion to the number of—(ANGELA *knocks on the study door*) Come in. The number of unfinished plays is in direct proportion . . . to the . . . number . . .
(*He trails off, gazing at the manuscript which* ANGELA *has laid on the desk before him*)

ANGELA I'm done.

PARKER With Act Two?

18

ANGELA With Act Three. Done. Finished. Complete.
(*A pause*)

PARKER (*Into recorder*) To be continued.
(*He puts aside the recorder*)

ANGELA Of course I'll have to do some rewriting, but I think it's—optionable.

PARKER *The Gingerbread World* . . .

ANGELA There were all kinds of Victorian trimming around the house, and it seemed sort of like a retreat from reality . . .

PARKER It's a nice title. I like it . . . *The Gingerbread World* . . .
(*A beat*)

ANGELA Read it.
(*A pause*)

PARKER Are you sure you want me to?

ANGELA You're the best critic in the whole apartment.
(*A smile between them, and then a pause*)

PARKER I won't lie, Angie. This isn't a cake or a hair-do or a slip cover.

ANGELA I don't want you to lie. And I don't think you'll have to. I think you're in for a surprise.

19

PARKER I hope so. I do.

>*(He holds up crossed fingers.* ANGELA *backs out of the study)*

ANGELA I'll be very quiet . . .*(She closes door as the light irises down to spot on* PARKER. *He lights a cigarette, draws on it, his eyes never leaving the waiting manuscript. After a moment he turns the title page, leans forward on one elbow and begins to read. The spot fades out and comes up on* ANGELA *in the living room, at the telephone)* Person-to-person to Washington, D.C. The number is District 7-4855, and I'd like to speak to Mrs. Charlotte Orr, O-R-R . . . Gramercy 7-3935 . . . Hello, Mom? Angela. How are you? . . . Fine, Mom. I finally finished it! Just this morning! . . . Thank you!! . . . Well, *thank you, darling!* Listen, I'm counting chickens before they're hatched, but could you possibly come take care of Park and John for three weeks or so, in the spring or maybe the fall? Essie can give us two extra days a week, but Park just gets *sick* over her cooking. He says she makes everything taste like dentists' fingers . . . Well, I may have to go out of town. S. P. Champlain is interested and if he decides to put it on . . . S. P. Champlain . . . Yes, the producer . . . Well, they *always* take them out of town first, to try them out and see how—to try them out— Oh, for Pete's sake. Mom, it's the *play* that I finished, not the scatter rug!!! *(Blackout. The spot comes up on* PARKER. *He reads the last few lines of the manuscript, closes it, and sits with his face in his hands. After a moment he emits a long, low, miserable moan. He opens the manuscript gingerly, peeks at one line, then quickly closes the manuscript, as though contagion might escape. Another moan. The lights come up in the living room.* ANGELA *is sitting as close to the study door as she can get.* JOHN's *coat and briefcase are on the couch.* JOHN *enters from the kitchen, eating a cookie*)

JOHN I'm going—

ANGELA Shh!

JOHN (*Whispering, as he takes his coat*) I'm going out. I'll be back in a few minutes.

ANGELA (*Whispering*) All right. (JOHN *quietly exits.* PARKER *rubs his eyes, sighing. He rises, picks up the manuscript, faces the door, draws a deep breath, and opens the door.* ANGELA *leaps to her feet and backs away, almost upsetting her chair*) I was—just sitting here—(PARKER *moves downstage, avoiding* ANGELA's *anxious eyes*) Well?

PARKER Angie . . . darling . . . I'm looking for an affirmative beginning . . . I keep coming back to the title. (*Facing her now*) It's a *good* title, Angie.

ANGELA But the play . . . ?

PARKER (*Shaking his head*) No, dear . . . No . . . I'm sorry. (*Clenches his fists and continues*) The characters are . . . sugar and spice and everything nice, but that's not what people are made of, not even little girls. These are . . . Kewpie dolls, all of them. And the dialogue is . . . clumsy, Angie. That's the only word. Except "pretentious" where I think you were trying to be poetic. The structure . . . ? There's none. This isn't a play at all, honey; it's a—a fuzzy, inexact memory; it hasn't been shaped or focused or organized or—or anything.
   (*A pause.* ANGELA *is white-faced, as though slapped*)

21

ANGELA How's the typing?

  (PARKER *extends the manuscript toward her*)

PARKER I'm sorry, Angie. I wish I could have said something else.

  (ANGELA *takes the manuscript. A beat*)

ANGELA Do you? Is that what you wish?

PARKER (*Tenderly taking her shoulders*) Angie baby, believe me, I wouldn't—

ANGELA (*On "believe," ruefully*) Suddenly I'm "Angie baby." For two and a half months you've been sticking pins in a little statue of me and now I'm "Angie baby."

PARKER Ah, don't, Angie . . .

ANGELA (*Drawing away*) It's true, isn't it? I've heard you wandering around, crooning your *voodoo* into that recorder . . .

PARKER (*Rigid*) The play is no good, Angie. You asked me to read it and I warned you, no lies.

ANGELA *Did* you read it? *I* don't think you read my play.

PARKER What does that mean?

ANGELA I think you read the play you were *hoping* I'd write, not the one I *did* write. I think I could have put—*Hamlet* in front of you, and all *you* would have seen would have been—one more mixed-up teen-ager with family problems!

PARKER (*Tight-jawed*) I read the play objectively, Angela.

ANGELA Objectively?

PARKER Yes, *objectively!* That happens to be my business! And I happen to be considered pretty good at it!

ANGELA No; not this time! No! This is a—a tender, simple, touching drama! It has *heart,* and it has *warmth,* and it has —it has *sweetness*—

PARKER Oh, it has sweetness, all right! Put that on a stage and you'll decay every tooth for ten miles around!

ANGELA Well, that is one man's opinion! (*At phone, takes a slip of note paper from her pocket, puts down the manuscript*) One man's biased, partial, prejudiced, one-sided opinion! (*Reading number, dialing phone*) Let's just see what S. P. Champlain will say! *He* isn't a self-satisfied male chauvinist who thinks a woman's place is in the broom closet! Nor does he tend to confuse himself with God and George Jean Nathan rolled into one! (*She completes dialing, waits*)

PARKER If Anthony Adverse answers, hang up.

ANGELA Mr. Champlain, please. Angela Ballantine. (*Hand over phone*) It just infuriates you, doesn't it, that I actually *finished* the play. The *Kitty Hawk* is up in the air now, and you're standing on the ground shouting, "It won't fly, it won't fly!"

PARKER The *Kitty Hawk?* Up in the air? (*Pointing at manuscript*) That—that HUPMOBILE?

ANGELA Mr. Champlain? How are you? . . . Just fine. Just wonderful. I'm finished, Mr. Champlain, and I couldn't be more pleased! (*Eyes on* PARKER) The characters, the dialogue, the structure; they're all *exactly* as I wanted them to be! I even like the typing! (*She laughs, then listens.* JOHN *enters*)

PARKER Go outside for a while, John.

JOHN I've just *been* outside! (*He comes downstage, listening, removing his coat*)

ANGELA Wonderful! . . . Yes . . . The fourth floor . . . And then you'll call? Wonderful, Mr. Champlain. (*Hangs up, picks up manuscript. With hauteur*) A messenger is coming for the script in fifteen minutes. (*She ascends the stairs and exits right*)

PARKER He'd better have cab fare because they'll never let him inside a bus with that thing. (*To* JOHN) Did you read it?

JOHN She kept it locked in the closet. And she hid the key.

PARKER I said "Did you read it."

JOHN Well, just the first act.

PARKER What did you think?

JOHN It was better than Dr. Von Hagedorn's first act . . . Like a broken arm is better than a broken back . . .

PARKER (*Muttering*) God and George Jean Nathan rolled into one . . .

JOHN (*Gesturing at phone*) Do you think he'll produce it?

PARKER Don't be ridiculous. (PARKER *exits into the study.* JOHN *takes his coat upstage.* ANGELA *enters, descends the stairs, fastening the manila envelope containing her manuscript.* JOHN *hangs his coat in the closet.* ANGELA *puts the envelope on the table and continues toward the kitchen*)

JOHN Angie . . . (ANGELA *stops.* JOHN *comes downstage to her*) Don't be angry with Dad. Please.
    (*A beat.* ANGELA *touches* JOHN's *arm, draws herself up coolly*)

ANGELA I'm not angry with him. If he chooses to despise my play, that's his privilege. Anger is an immature emotion, and I like to think I've outgrown it. I'm not angry; not angry in the least.

JOHN You're hurting my arm . . .
    (ANGELA *breathes a quick "I'm sorry," kisses* JOHN's *arm, and exits into the kitchen as the lights fade out. The spot comes up in study.* PARKER *is at the desk, dictating irritably into recorder*)

PARKER Monday, February—oh, twenty-second, twenty-third; *I* don't know! Notes for book: "Don't Write That Play"; Chapter Fourteen. So your play is optioned. So the announcements have been published, and the phone has been

ringing, and there hasn't been a moment's peace in a whole
damn month! Cut "damn." And now, gentle reader, you
think your troubles are over? Ha-ha! They *begin,* my friend,
they *begin!* A producer was *easy* to find; anyone with a dime
and a phone booth and the telephone number of a man
with money is a producer! But now you need a *director.*
Without a skillful, energetic director to tear your play
apart and punch it back together again, to tear a dozen
actors apart and punch *them* back together again, without
such a man you are lost, my neophyte; and the skillful,
energetic directors, you will soon learn, are both busy. (*The
lights come up in the living room*) What you will find
available instead of energy will be sterility; the tired me-
chanic who was directed seven thousand plays—

> (*During this,* ANGELA *enters through the front door,
> wearing a coat and holding a bound manuscript. With
> excitedly flushed cheeks, she ushers in* DION KAPAKOS, *a
> hatless, hot-eyed* wunderkind *of twenty-nine or thirty,
> very skillful and energetic-looking. He strides downstage,
> checking over the room as though he has just bought it*)

DION Nice, nice, nice. Nice. Nice.
> (*He opens his woodsman's coat and rubs his hands
> with restless vitality. Under the coat he wears a heavy
> knitted turtleneck sweater and dungarees.* ANGELA *goes
> to the study door*)

PARKER (*Continuing over the above without a break*)—and
lost somewhere along the way whatever vibrant enthusiasm
he may have possessed in his greener years. Instead of skill
there will be available only the automatic hack work of
Hollywood has-beens, or the lifeless, checkerboard staging
of men so complacent in their established authority, so

26

gross with the gross receipts of their past successes, that any
new and dynamic attack is as far beyond their powers as—
(ANGELA *knocks on "far"*)

ANGELA Parker!

PARKER Yo?

ANGELA There's someone here I'd like you to meet.
(PARKER *puts down the recorder, rises, and opens the
door*)

PARKER Hi.

ANGELA Park, this is Dion Kapakos.
(*A beat, then* PARKER *goes enthusiastically to* DION)

PARKER Well . . . hello!

DION How are you, sir!
(*They shake hands warmly, while* ANGELA *beams*)

PARKER I've been hoping we'd run into each other!

DION Same here, sir, same here!

PARKER Someone told me you had a beard!

DION I did! But it was just insecurity. One hit show and out
came the old razor.
(*All laugh*)

ANGELA (*Sweetly*) Dion is going to direct *Gingerbread*.
(PARKER *gapes*) He was my first choice; I remembered all

27

those wonderful things you said about him last season. (PARKER *still gapes.* ANGELA *smiles complacently on* DION) "The drive and thrust of a jet-engine . . ."

DION   You know, I wrote you a three-page letter, sir, after that review of *Oh, Doctor!*

PARKER   I don't remember—

DION   I tore it up. It was—too damn slushy. You're kind of like a father image for me. It's true; I'm an arrogant little snot and you're just about the only man alive whose opinion I really respect. I mean that. The other critics? Hell, you throw a serious drama at them, it's like—throwing a medicine ball at a baby. And comedies? Ha! Half of them don't know their *farce* from a hole in the ground!
   (DION *grins;* ANGELA *laughs;* PARKER *can't quite make it*)

PARKER   You're going to direct—
   (*A gesture at the manuscript in* ANGELA'S *hand*)

DION   Love at first sight. The minute I finished reading it I called my agent and burned my bridges. I was all set to do the musical version of *David Copperfield,* you know.

PARKER   I heard . . .

DION   (*Striding around*)   But I've *had* musicals. *Oh, Doctor!* was just a way to get off the summer circuit. *Drama* is my meat. I'm Greek, you know. Kapakos? That is, my grandfather was Greek. From Epidaurus, where the amphitheatre is. I went back there last summer, sat on those stone steps in the moonlight . . . I found *roots* there, I really did.
   (*A beat*)

28

ANGELA You two talk; I'll get the notes.
  (*She goes up the stairs*)

PARKER Notes?

DION On *Gingerbread*. I want to go over all the stuff Angela
  discarded. We're going to do a full rewrite, from the ground
  up. (ANGELA *exits right*) Hey, would you mind telling me
  where you find a girl like that? Beauty, sensitivity, mod-
  esty . . .

PARKER Random House, but they're out of stock.

DION Yessir, she and I have *work* ahead of us! And rehearsals
  in just four weeks! That's March twenty-second, then New
  Haven, April thirteenth; Boston, April nineteenth; New
  York, May third.

PARKER Champlain moves fast . . .

DION He's a producer. A real one. You know, some of them
  have no talent at all; just a dime and the phone number of
  a money-man.

PARKER Mmm . . .

DION Benson Hedgeman is pretty well set for Uncle Ben.
  Perfect casting, isn't it? His arm is clean as a whistle; hasn't
  been *near* the stuff in over a year.

PARKER Say, do you . . . *really think* Angie has—Greek
  drama there?

DION Not now, but wait till I'm finished with it. Between
  you and me, that script of hers is carrying fifty pounds of

fat in all the wrong places, and it's wrapped up in tinsel and ribbons up to its eyeballs. Inside, though, it has bones; fine, lean bones. It's like a big fat overdressed woman. Me, I'm Slenderella.

PARKER   Personally, I think it's a job for Mandrake the Magician.

DION   Oh, I know; Angela told me how *you* feel. *You* I would *love* to make a monkey out of!

PARKER   Overthrow the father image?

DION (*Grinning*)   Sort of.

PARKER   Well, you *did* pull off one miracle with *Oh, Doctor!* . . . If ever I walked into a theatre thinking I was stepping aboard the *Titanic,* that was the night.

DION   Now wait, don't give *me* all the credit. *Oh, Doctor!* was built on the best foundation of any musical in the past five years. There aren't many novels around that can top *Arrowsmith,* you know.
   (ANGELA *enters right with the manila folder, descends the stairs*)

ANGELA   I got together whatever I could find, but it doesn't add up to very much.

DION (*Going to her*)   It'll all help. We have to go right back to the *roots* of the play.
   (*He takes the folder, looks in it*)

PARKER Where are you working?

DION My place. I have a hole in the wall over on Bleecker Street. In the phone book, if you're the nervous type.
(*A sly grin*)

PARKER I'm not. Opening tonight, Angie. Early dinner.

ANGELA I know.

DION Oh, she'll be early. Today we just shake hands and promise no fouls; tomorrow is round one. (*Closes the folder, crosses to* PARKER) It's been a pleasure meeting you, sir. It really has.
(*They shake hands*)

PARKER You can drop the "sir" if you'd like; I missed the Civil War by a good five years.

DION Sorry; I guess it's the father-image bit. Parker—
(*He offers his hand again*)

PARKER (*Shaking it*) Dion.
(DION *joins* ANGELA *at foyer. She holds the manuscript clasped to her bosom*)

DION Ready for the fray? (ANGELA *nods solemnly.* DION *taps the manuscript*) This is just the *beginning* of a play, girlie, but—(*Turning to* PARKER, *grinning*)—you know what *I* always say?

PARKER I'll bite; *what* do you always say?

DION "A playwright's reach should exceed his grasp, or what's New Haven for?" Ha, ha, ha, ha . . .

(*All laugh.* DION *takes* ANGELA's *arm; they exit.* PARKER *watches them off. He turns, looking puzzled, as the lights fade. The lights come up in the living room.* JOHN *enters through the front door, wearing a coat, suit, and necktie. He looks terribly sad*)

JOHN   Dad? (*Morosely hangs away the coat. Louder*) Dad? (*The study door opens.* PARKER *looks out*)

PARKER   How was it?

JOHN (*Coming downstage*)   Awful. I should never have asked Angie to let me in. I should have kept my mouth shut and gone to a movie.

PARKER   Lots of first run-throughs are pretty bad. It's practically a tradition.

JOHN   Not like this; it *couldn't* be.

PARKER (*Coming into the living room*)   What has Kapakos done to the script?

JOHN   It's worse than it was before. The roomers in the boarding house, they're like a Greek chorus now. They stand at the side of the stage and *chant* things.

PARKER   Oh, God . . .

JOHN   At the end, when everybody leaves, Uncle Ben shoots himself.

PARKER   No . . .

32

JOHN   And they changed the title; it's not *The Gingerbread World* any more, it's *A Houseful of Silence*.

PARKER   Oh, Lord . . . (*Paces, then strikes his palm angrily*) The fool! The damn fool! That man had the makings of a first-rate director! First-rate! And then he had to go sit on the steps of an amphitheatre in the moonlight! Are you *sure* it's that bad? Who else was there?

JOHN   There was a cleaning woman sitting near me.

PARKER   Did she listen?

JOHN   For five minutes. Then she said, "Why should I be sitting here when I can be doing the men's room," and she went out.

PARKER   Oh, Lord . . . How's Angie taking it?

JOHN   (*Sitting on the couch*) She looks worried. They *all* look worried, except Mr. Kapakos. (PARKER *paces*) Angie asked me what I thought about it. I said, "I'm a kid; what do *I* know?"

PARKER   In June, when the season's dead, we're going to take her to Paris. That's the one thing she's always wanted. I'll switch around my vacation. If I can't, I'll take a leave-of-absence.

JOHN   Dad . . .

PARKER   What?

JOHN   Are you going to review it? When it opens in New York? *A Houseful of Silence?*

PARKER *If* it opens, you mean. I think so. I'm not sure.

JOHN Would you tell the truth?

PARKER No, I would lie, the way I always do.

JOHN All right, don't get sore . . .

PARKER Well, what kind of question is that; would I tell the truth . . .

JOHN (*Worried*) It's going to be like Ivy all over again . . .

PARKER Now, look—

JOHN (*A sudden frightened anger*) Well, you told the truth about Ivy, didn't you?
(*A beat.* PARKER *sits beside* JOHN)

PARKER Now, look. There is nothing for you to get—scared about. There are good marriages and there are bad marriages. Ivy and I had a bad one. For nine years we piled up unhappiness between us, and it was all those tons of *unhappiness* that caused our divorce, *not my review of her Helen of Troy.* The review may have been the spark, but the nine years of unhappiness were the gunpowder. Are you with me? (JOHN *is listening very intently, but he doesn't nod yet*) Angie and I have a *good* marriage. If I say bad things about *Gingerbread* she may—

JOHN *A Houseful of Silence.*

PARKER If I say bad things about *A Houseful of Silence,* Angie may be hurt, and angry with me. But there *ain't no gunpowder* in this apartment. A good marriage doesn't break up like a ten-cent glider; you got that? (JOHN *nods*) Okay . . . (*Rises, patting* JOHN's *hand*) Now go eat a cookie. (*He starts toward the study*)

JOHN I still don't see why you can't let someone *else* write the review . . .

    (PARKER *stops, turns, takes a deep exasperated breath*)

PARKER Who? Harvey Rittenhouse?

JOHN He's not *that* bad . . .

PARKER Harvey Rittenhouse is a blithering idiot who sits in those off-Broadway theatres and sees nothing but *me* walking into an open manhole! Not while I'm breathing will I hand him the reins, and especially not for *A Houseful of Moonlit Greek Amphitheatres!* He's just ass enough to be polite about it.

JOHN What if he is? What difference does it make?
    (*A beat*)

PARKER A spade ought to be called a spade . . .

JOHN And you don't *care* if you hurt Angie and make her angry . . .

PARKER Sure I care! What do you think I am; Bluebeard? (*Crouches down beside couch*) John, listen . . . Sometimes you *have* to hurt people. Even people you love . . . If I lie about Angie's play, or if I get off the hook by letting Harvey Rittenhouse cover it—I'm going to lose a good-size piece of my self-respect. Maybe a piece of my self-respect

35

sounds tiny compared to hurting Angie, but if I start disliking myself a little, I'm going to start disliking the *whole world* a little, Angie included. And you. You're both sharp; you'll sense that, and *you'll* start disliking *me* a little. And I'll sense *that* and bingo!—there we are, in the worst kind of vicious circle there ever was. I know it from experience. And you do too. Remember the—old crank I was four or five years ago? And the little crumb that *you* were? (JOHN *nods soberly.* PARKER *rises from his crouching position*) Never sell off a piece of yourself just to avoid hurting someone. The people who matter will understand and forgive, and the people who *can't* understand and forgive— well, they don't matter.

(*A pause*)

JOHN (*Looking up at him*) Boy, that's the biggest thing you ever told me, isn't it?

PARKER Bet your life it is.

JOHN Except about sex, maybe.
(PARKER *laughs*)

PARKER Hey, you know what? I'll bet you five bucks *A Houseful of Silence* never even gets on the trail.

JOHN You really think so?

PARKER If the run-through was as bad as you say, Champlain isn't going to pour away *more* money, is he?

JOHN Is it *his* own money?
(*The lights slowly iris down to a spot on* PARKER *and* JOHN)

PARKER It's *money,* never mind whose. He isn't going to pour it away, is he?

JOHN I guess not . . .

PARKER I'll *bet* not! Never! It's going to be rough on Angie, though . . .

JOHN No New Haven . . .

PARKER We're going to have to treat her like a princess.

JOHN Help her get over the disappointment.

PARKER She's worked so—darn hard . . .
(*The spot fades out as a second spot comes up on the bedroom door.* ANGELA, *in a traveling suit, plants a large, heavy suitcase on the landing and steps back into the bedroom. After a moment she reappears, with a smaller suitcase and a hatbox, and puts them down*)

ANGELA (*Calling off right*) And if your father takes you to any of the openings you do your homework first, you hear?

JOHN (*Off*) I hear!
(ANGELA *takes her coat and purse from a chair within the bedroom door*)

ANGELA And if you happen not to like whatever play it is, you just sit there quietly. None of that *groaning* business!
(*She picks up the hatbox, and comes downstairs. As she descends, late afternoon light comes up in the living room.* PARKER *is lying on the couch*)

37

PARKER (*Holding recorder as a microphone*) All ashore that's going ashore. Whooooooo . . . (ANGELA, *paying him no attention, puts down the hatbox and coat, opens her purse, takes out a pencil and a slip of paper, crosses out something*) When is train time?

ANGELA We're not taking the train; we're driving. Dion has an MG.

PARKER He would . . .

ANGELA (*Next item on her list*) Now remember, Mom's train gets in at Penn Station, not Grand Central. Ten fifty-five Monday morning.

PARKER I'll have the band there at ten-thirty, just to be safe.

ANGELA Tell her I'll call Monday night.

PARKER Check.

ANGELA There's food inside for tonight, and you can take John out tomorrow night. I left a list of stores for Mom. On the refrigerator.

PARKER Check.
    (*A beat*)

ANGELA She'll spoil you, you'll see. She runs a home ten times better than I *ever* will.

PARKER That I doubt.
    (*A beat*)

ANGELA Tell her to watch out for the short butcher, the one who has to lean on the scale.

(She pantomimes, craning up to read an imaginary dial while pressing where the tray would be)

PARKER *(Into recorder, à la Dick Tracy)* Watch out for short butcher. That is all.
(A beat. They smile. PARKER sits up)

ANGELA *(Putting purse on hatbox)* Well, I'd better . . .
(She goes up the stairs. PARKER puts the recorder on the table, and rises)

PARKER Wait, I'll get the big one. *(ANGELA is coming down-stairs with the smaller suitcase as PARKER ascends. He puts his hand across to the banister, blocking her. They look at each other, then kiss twice; husband-wife kisses; nothing orgasmic)* I was beginning to forget little off-the-cuff kisses . . .

ANGELA *(Touching him)* Park . . . *(The doorbell rings)* It's Dion. *(They kiss again, then PARKER goes up and ANGELA down. The doorbell rings again—impatiently)* Coming!
(ANGELA puts down the suitcase and goes to the front door, as PARKER picks up the large suitcase and starts down. ANGELA opens the door. DION enters, picks up ANGELA by the waist, whirls her around and carries her downstage, singing over her cries of "Dion! Put me down! Dion!")

DION
"Off we go, into the wild blue yonder,
Climbing high, into the sun
Into the sun, hey!"
(He puts ANGELA down and thrusts a hand at PARKER,

who has just put down the large suitcase and is look-
ing somewhat undelighted)

DION Hiya! Don't mind me! (*Shakes* PARKER's *hand*) I get
this way at this stage of the game! All front; underneath it
I'm scared silly! Knees like water!

ANGELA (*Straightening herself, muttering*) We haven't even
left yet and I'm worn out . . .
(JOHN *appears on the landing, watching*)

DION Don't worry; I've got a glove compartment full of
Benzedrine and caffein pills. Hey, there's that Johnny-boy
who was at the run-through! How ya doin', Johnny-boy?

JOHN (*Coming down a few steps*) Fine . . .

DION (*To* PARKER) Wonderful kid! I love kids! We *communi-
cate!*

PARKER With two tin cans and a long string?

DION Ha, ha, ha, ha! Hey, Angie, did you ask him?

ANGELA No. I thought I would wait until you—

DION Park—

PARKER Yes, Di?
(*A beat.* DION *smiles uncertainly*)

DION We're having a bit of trouble, Angie and I. Champlain
has got producer-itis. He's trying to bully us into using a
new third act that he's dreamed up with some cretin of a
script reader. I think it's the third act of *Bertha, the Sewing-*

Henry Fonda as PARKER BALLANTINE

Machine Girl. On top of that we have to break in a new Uncle Ben. Turns out Benson Hedgeman has been junked all along and now he's *really* flying.

PARKER   I thought you said his arm was clean as a whistle.

DION   It is. He's been shooting the stuff into his *leg,* the damn sneak.

ANGELA   Dion and I would like you to come up to New Haven for a couple of days next week. There are no openings after Wednesday night.

DION   And Boston too, if you've got a few days around the twenty-fifth. Just to look at things and drop a suggestion here and there.
(*A beat*)

PARKER   I'm sorry; I can't do that.

ANGELA   Why not?

PARKER   If I contribute something to the play, how can I review it? It's going to be hard enough to be objective as it is.

ANGELA   How can you re—?

DION   You're going to *review* it?

PARKER   Yes, I am. I've talked it over with my editor, and myself, and I'm going to.

DION   We assumed you would—disqualify yourself.

PARKER   Sorry, I'm a vampire; nothing disqualifies *me* but a stake through the heart.

41

JOHN Or being caught outside the coffin in direct sunlight.

PARKER *(To* DION, *pointing back over his shoulder at* JOHN) The world's leading authority on vampires.

ANGELA But—but that's not *fair!* You *read* the play! You *hated* it!

PARKER I'd review it if I loved it. I'll do my best to be objective.

DION But damn it, she's your *wife!*

PARKER No, she isn't, not on opening night. *(To* ANGELA) You're a playwright, I'm a critic; let's both do our jobs as well as we can, and shake hands before and after.

ANGELA *Surgeons* don't *operate* on their wives!

PARKER I'm not going to *operate,* Angie; I'm going to look at a play and write an opinion on it.

DION Can't you forget you're a critic for a couple of weeks and give us a hand?

PARKER No, I can't.

ANGELA Oh no, not he! He *never* forgets he's a critic! Not even on his wedding night!

PARKER Angie, if you're going to dig up that old—

ANGELA Do you know what he did? Do you know what this witty, perceptive—

PARKER It was a *joke,* Angie!

ANGELA Oh sure, a joke! The morning after our wedding! Do you know what he did?

PARKER (*Striding away*) Holy mackerel . . . !

ANGELA The morning after our wedding. I woke up. He was in the shower. There was a note on the pillow next to me. Do you know what it said? (DION *shakes his head.* ANGELA *sets each word up on an imaginary billboard*) " 'A memorable evening'—Parker Ballantine"!

PARKER It was a joke. You laughed for five minutes.

ANGELA Sure I laughed! Even in the Chinese water torture the first few drops tickle a little! Not once have you forgot you're a critic! You've been sitting in judgment on me day and night for nineteen months! Criticizing me for not being a good enough housekeeper, criticizing me for—

PARKER (*On latter "criticizing"*) When have I ever criticized you? I've *never* criticized!

ANGELA Always! Criticizing me for not finishing that damn scatter rug, criticizing me for not having a baby . . .
    (*A beat*)

PARKER I have never criticized you, Angie. *You* are your critic, not I.

ANGELA And now you're going to step on my play . . . One thing I've done, one thing I've accomplished, and *you're* going to grind it under that witty, perceptive heel of yours!

43

PARKER I'll call it as I see it. It's my work. I have to do it.

DION (*Taking up* ANGELA's *coat, holding it up behind her*) Come on, Angie. He doesn't want to help, we'll do it without him.

ANGELA (*Moving away from* DION, *toward* PARKER) How noble you make it sound! "It's my work. I have to do it." And is that your work too? (*Pointing at the recorder on the table*) All that phony-baloney "Don't Write That Play"? That snide, oily sarcasm? I've heard you! "You'll never finish Act One, you'll never get a producer, you'll never get a director . . ."

DION (*Coming up again with the coat*) Come on, Angie. Don't let him get you. That's the girl . . .

ANGELA (*Allowing* DION *to put the coat on her*) A critic is supposed to point *up*, not *down*, you—you hatchet-man! "You'll never get into rehearsal, you'll never get out of town . . ."

DION (*Putting purse and hatbox into* ANGELA's *hands*) Let's go, honey . . .

ANGELA You know, Shakespeare's first play was an amateur's work too, Mr. Ballantine!
(*A pause.* PARKER *is silent*)

DION Let's go . . . Please . . . Angie, damn it, I'm *double-parked* . . .

PARKER I'm sorry, Angie, but I've got to review your play, and review it truthfully. I've lied and evaded before. Six

times. For Ivy. I can't do it again. It's a question of . . .
keeping my self-respect . . .

ANGELA *Keep* your self-respect! I don't want it! Just—just
quit hijacking mine!
(*On the edge of tears, she runs out.* DION *picks up her
two suitcases, goes to the door, turns and faces* PARKER)

DION She and I are coming back into town with the best
damn play you've ever seen.

PARKER Who's in the suitcase; Tennessee Williams?
(DION *exits.* PARKER *moves downstage.* JOHN *comes down
a few steps*)

JOHN Are you *sure* there's no gunpowder in this apartment?

PARKER Go eat a cookie.

JOHN I never saw Angie like that . . . (*Coming down the
remaining steps*) I don't like that Dion Kapakos . . . I
don't like the way he called me "Johnny-boy," and the way
he helped Angie on with her coat. He made it look as if he
were helping her on with . . . I don't know, some kind of
a *bathrobe* . . .

PARKER In thirty seconds we're going to have "Spank-the-Precocious-Children Hour."

JOHN What did I say? Didn't you see the way he sort of
rubbed—

PARKER (*On* "*sort*") Go eat a cookie! Go on!
(*A beat.* JOHN *crosses quickly to the kitchen door,
glances at* PARKER's *back, exits.* PARKER *strikes his palm,*

45

takes a breath, swallows a portion of his anger. He snaps up the recorder, holds it as though he might throw it, then weighs it on his palm, his lips clenched. He calms; his eyes cloud. He turns a knob on the recorder and flips a switch. There is a continuous low buzzing sound. With the recorder on his palm, PARKER *sits in a low chair. He watches the humming instrument dourly.* JOHN *enters from the kitchen, eating a cookie. He stands near* PARKER)

JOHN Erasing?

PARKER Yeah, I'm going to erase the whole business. She hit it on the nose. Snide, oily sarcasm, pointing down, not up. Precious, as you said in the very beginning.
(*A beat*)

JOHN But gee . . . it's a few months' work . . .

PARKER Big deal . . .
(*A pause. The recorder buzzes on.* JOHN *and* PARKER *watch it*)

JOHN You know what's in the refrigerator?

PARKER What?

JOHN TV dinners.
(PARKER *sinks lower in his chair with a miserable "Oh, boy" as*

The Curtain Falls

ACT TWO

ACT TWO

At rise, the living room is bright with afternoon light. At the desk in the study, PARKER *sits reading by dim lamplight. The study door is closed.*

The telephone rings; once, then again, then a third time.

PARKER *is deaf to the ringing.* ESSIE, *a Negro woman, enters from the kitchen. She is in a hat, coat, and dress; her work finished. She carries an old canvas satchel, which she puts down near the foyer before answering the phone on the fourth or fifth ring.*

ESSIE Good afternoon, Ballantine residence. This is the maid ... Yes, Mr. Ballantine's here, but he's got himself locked up in his study and don't want to be disturbed ... Mrs. Ballantine? *She's* up at the theatre on Forty-fourth Street. They're having one last rehearsal before the big opening of her play tonight ... Well, Mrs. Orr is here. That's Mrs. Ballantine's mother that's been here three or four weeks now. She's upstairs in the guest room, resting ... John is still at school ... Do you want me to get Mrs. Orr? ... Oh. Well, who should I say called? Hello? Ma'am? Hello? *(Looks at receiver, shrugs, hangs it up, and mutters)* Crazy phone calls in this apartment ...

(She picks up her satchel and goes out the front door, and that's the last we see of ESSIE *until the curtain calls. After a moment* CHARLOTTE ORR *comes down the stairs. She is an attractive and smartly dressed woman who looks as though she could improve the management of Lord & Taylor and still have her afternoons free)*

CHARLOTTE (*Knocking on study door*) Parker, may I speak with you for a minute or two, please?

PARKER I'm working, Charlie.

CHARLOTTE No, you're not, dear, you're reading Agatha Christie. (PARKER's *resigned shrug confirms this*) Now come on, don't be stubborn; come out of your filing cabinet. (CHARLOTTE *moves away and adjusts the level of a few pictures.* PARKER *rises, unlocks and opens the door*) I'll say this for that girl Essie; she's not much trouble to straighten up after. Come on, take a breather. Once you've read fifty Agatha Christies you've read them all.

PARKER (*Coming into the living room*) Ahh, I'm just looking for a foolproof way to bump off Lillian Hellman and Clare Boothe Luce.
(*He sits disconsolately on the couch*)

CHARLOTTE And if it works on them you use it on Angela, right?

PARKER Right.

CHARLOTTE Poor Parker . . .

PARKER It ought to be part of the unwritten law; any man who catches his wife alone with a typewriter—pow!
(*He fires his forefinger, then blows the smoke from its muzzle and holsters it*)

CHARLOTTE I had hoped that when she got back from Boston a truce would be negotiated. (*Indicating the bedroom*) Up in—headquarters.

PARKER (*Shaking his head*) No, the barbed wire is still strung clear across the room. And you can guess which piece of furniture it cuts right through the middle of.

CHARLOTTE (*Sitting*) Parker, have I put my nose into this business *once* during the weeks I've been here? Have I lectured you or pushed you or given you even a *pinch* of advice?

PARKER No, you haven't.

CHARLOTTE I may have been a lousy mother but I am the best damn mother-in-law in existence.

PARKER I don't imagine you were such a lousy mother, Charlie.

CHARLOTTE Believe me, Parker, I was. The proof is in the puddingheads. In my fever to be mother *and* father to those poor girls I stifled all three of them, not just Angela. My deadly efficiency; I didn't even let them lick their own stamps! And look at them today. Angela in New York; married, but scared stiff she can't fulfill a woman's role. Sally in Paris; *she's* fulfilling a woman's role, all right, even by *French* standards, only she's not married. And Marge in *Kyoto* . . . the first non-Japanese ever to take the full twenty-year course in flower arranging . . . Now that I've got you smiling, Parker, I'm going to give you some advice.

PARKER Charlie . . .

CHARLOTTE I am, and you're going to listen! Being the ideal mother-in-law is all well and good, but ten minutes ago, up in my room, it suddenly dawned upon me just *why* mothers-in-law are always lecturing and pushing and giving advice to their sons-in-law. It's because we *know more,* that's why!

PARKER (*Yielding with amusement*) I give up. What's the advice?

CHARLOTTE This evening, when we leave for the theatre, you take that little white box of yours and put some of the slips in your right-hand pocket and the rest of the slips in your left-hand pocket. That's all.
(*A beat.* PARKER *shakes his head*)

PARKER No. Mm-mnn. One pocket white, one pocket black; the same as always.

CHARLOTTE You're a fool.

PARKER Charlie, I saw your face when you came back from that preview last night! You looked as though you'd swallowed a dish of raw sweetbreads!

CHARLOTTE All right, it's *not* the best play that's ever been written . . . (PARKER *fixes her with a juryman's gaze. She shifts*) I'll even allow it isn't a very *good* play . . . That critic in Boston, how did he put it? "Fair-to-maudlin."

PARKER That critic in Boston is one of my closest friends and a gentleman of the old school, the one Sir Walter Raleigh attended.

CHARLOTTE Oh, Lord, you're going to make me come right out and say it, aren't you? All right, the play stinks. I sat there in that audience and I wanted to *apologize* to all those poor people. Even the ones who were there on passes.

PARKER (*Rising*) One pocket white, one pocket black.

CHARLOTTE Lie a little! No one will execute you! Women will admire you, men will feel compassion! And maybe Angela will understand once and for all how much you love her. That wouldn't hurt, you know.

PARKER Charlie, I'm a nut, I know I am, but I still have *nightmares* once in a while about those fake reviews I wrote to keep Ivy happy. And when I say nightmares, Charlie, I mean pajama-soakers! I'm in a plane, a passenger plane, flying over mountains. The stewardess comes around with cocktails, and those six reviews are printed on the little napkins. Suddenly everybody is ugly-drunk and coming at me with their knives and forks. "Look, folks, look, I told the truth about *Helen of Troy!*" And then the pilot comes out, played by my high-school English teacher, and he taps me on the shoulder and informs me that we're overweight and one passenger has to jump . . .

CHARLOTTE Good grief, I can imagine what *your* upbringing must have been . . . !

PARKER (*Smiling*) A montage of hairbrushes and whistling belts. It gave me standards of right and wrong, though.

CHARLOTTE Fine. Now, where are you going to look for your *third* wife, at Simon and Schuster?

PARKER Charlie . . .

53

CHARLOTTE (*Urgently*) Angela ran away from home once before, don't forget!

PARKER She isn't running anywhere. Believe me, you know the girl, I know the woman. She's going to stay right *here*.

CHARLOTTE Parker, please, listen to— (*The doorbell rings*) Ohh . . . (CHARLOTTE *rises and starts for the door.* PARKER *heads for the study*) You stay away from that study; I'm not through with you yet!
    (CHARLOTTE *opens the door*)

IVY How do you do. I'd like to see Mr. Bal—

PARKER Ivy! For God's sake—!

IVY (*Sweeping in*) Parker-Love! How *are* you!
    (*She kisses* PARKER *exuberantly on his reddening cheek, while* CHARLOTTE *stares, still holding the door open.* IVY LONDON *is glossy, electric, glamorous, and admits to thirty-four years. She is carrying a cosmetics case and wearing a slack suit under her swirling coat of horizontal-stripe mink*)

PARKER What on earth are you—

IVY (*Whirling away*) Visiting, love, just visiting! What a *heaven* apartment! You must be taking *bribes,* darling! And look! A loom! Angela weaves! How clever of her!
    (*Now* CHARLOTTE *slams the door*)

PARKER Ivy—Charlie, this is Ivy London. Ivy; Charlotte Orr, Angela's mother.

IVY Charlotte Orr? A decorator? Washington?

CHARLOTTE Yes.

IVY (*Seizing* CHARLOTTE's *hand*) But I *love* you! You did
Lissy Ramarandhi's apartment! Where oh where did you
get those marvelous ivory masks? I've been searching every-
where for them! Here, Washington, Dallas—

CHARLOTTE There's a little shop in Johannesburg . . .
     (*This creates a small breech, into which* PARKER *man-
     fully jumps*)

PARKER I thought your show was in Boston, Ivy.

IVY Oh it was, darling, but we folded. Like little Arabs. Or
is it the tents that fold? Anyway we died. A horrible death.
They all but threw the usherettes at us. (*Drops the cosmetics
case, shucks off her coat*) God, I'm exhausted! I just came
from the train. May I sit? (*Sits as she asks*) Oh, you were
right, Parker! You were right! When oh when will I learn
to listen to you? There are some books that simply cannot be
made into musical comedies and *Twenty Thousand Leagues
Under the Sea* is one of them!

CHARLOTTE You came visiting directly from the train?

IVY Yes. Well, there *is* something I have to discuss with
Parker . . .
     (*A beat*)

CHARLOTTE If you'll excuse me, I think I'll take a little nap.
     (*She goes to the stairs*)

55

PARKER   You don't have to, Charlie.

CHARLOTTE   (*Ascending*)   It's been a pleasure meeting you, Miss London.

IVY   My pleasure, Mrs. Orr.

CHARLOTTE   (*On the landing*)   I admired you when I first saw you in *Kiss Me Good-bye,* and since then I haven't missed one of your Washington engagements. It's heartwarming to see that your vivacity isn't only stagecraft and that your beauty is more than makeup and amber lights.
   (*She exits right*)

IVY   She hates me.

PARKER   What are you talking about? That was the nicest speech anyone ever made to you.

IVY   It was in code; you pick out every other word and you get the real message.

PARKER   Well, it was damn thoughtless of you to come bursting in this way, today of all days. Angie might have been here, and seeing you would hardly have helped her opening-night nerves.

IVY   Don't growl, Parker-Love. I made sure the coast was clear before I came.

PARKER   Made sure?

IVY   Yes, I did. And by the way, you have without a doubt the most talkative maid this side of the New Dramatists League.

PARKER (*Sitting*) All right, what do we have to discuss that rates a personal appearance?

IVY Please, let me catch my breath. I still have Boston in my lungs. How's John?

PARKER Dynamite.

IVY I saw Angela in Boston; did she tell you?

PARKER No.

IVY We overlapped. My company came in a week before hers left. We were all at the same hotel; her company, my company, and one other company that was in town too. It was a madhouse. There's no people like show people, all right; depraved, lascivious, corrupt . . . The goings-on! I tell you, that place was simply a hotbed of—hot beds. Angela, though, looked wonderfully radiant.

PARKER She always does.

IVY And dear Dion Kapakos, the scourge of the summer theatres. The barns that faun has chased me through! I'm not bragging, darling; you know young genius types; it's either one little boy or every woman in sight. Of course the girls in our company found him rather preoccupied last week, what with all sorts of conferences, and long meetings in the wee small hours . . .

PARKER Ivy . . . I can't thank you enough for this vivid picture of life on the road . . . But if there's something you want to discuss, get to it. I happen to be in the middle of some extremely important work.

(*He gestures toward the study*)

IVY My, you *are* inhospitable. It's been at least six months since we've seen each other, and all you can think of is— John! Johnny-Love!

(JOHN *has entered during the above line; in a zipper jacket, carrying a briefcase. A beat*)

JOHN Hello.

PARKER Ivy's come to pay us a little visit.

IVY Come here! Let me look at you! (JOHN *puts down the brief case, comes downstage*) My God, you're enormous! You're a giant! (*Taking* JOHN's *hands*) How old are you now? No, no! Never mind! Never mind! Give me a kiss. (JOHN *still loves* IVY *a little, despite the casual way he can speak of her. It shows in the shyness with which he kisses her and receives her kiss. She holds him off at arm's length*) My, oh my, oh my! At least we achieved one good thing between us, didn't we, Parker?

PARKER Oh, he's all right, I guess.

JOHN How are you?

IVY Wonderful, darling.

JOHN Is your show coming in?

IVY No, lamb, it's gone out, *way* out.

JOHN I'm sorry.

IVY Of course you are, sweet. Everybody is sorry, except Jules Verne. (*She releases* JOHN's *hands. He unzips his jacket and removes it*) Do you have some cottage cheese around by any chance? I'm ravenous. Couldn't get a thing on the train; the dining car was all full of Egyptians or Shriners or something. Do you have some? Cottage cheese?
    (*A beat*)

PARKER Probably . . .

IVY Johnny-Love, do you think I could have a dab of it? Just about enough to put under a microscope?
    (JOHN *looks to* PARKER)

PARKER Sure . . .

JOHN Sure.
    (*He goes to the kitchen*)

IVY With a dash of pepper, darling.

JOHN Okay.
    (*He exits*)

IVY *What* are you *feeding* him? He's grown three full inches!

PARKER We don't feed him anything. Angie grabs one end; I grab the other; and we pull.
    (*A smile between them*)

IVY I miss you so much . . .

PARKER I miss you too, on my masochistic days.

IVY (*A protest*) Parker ...

PARKER Come on, don't get sentimental just because you've had a flop. What did you come here to talk about?
(*A beat*)

IVY Something that isn't easy to say ...

PARKER Try a simple declarative sentence; a subject, a verb, an object.

IVY All right ... Well, Dion is the subject, and Angela's the object. The verb, I'm afraid, is rather Anglo-Saxon. (PARKER *doesn't blink; he just sits looking at* IVY) It's true, my darling. It was all over the hotel. Bring me a Bible and I'll swear on it.
(*Still no reaction from* PARKER. JOHN *enters from the kitchen with a plate of cottage cheese and a fork.* PARKER *and* IVY, *eyes locked, seem not to notice*)

JOHN Here's the cottage cheese.

PARKER Hold the plate over her head and tilt it forward.
(JOHN *stares at him*)

IVY Daddy's joking, darling. (*Takes the plate from* JOHN's *hand*) Thank you.
(*She eats a nibble of cheese*)

PARKER John, are you still *persona non grata* down at the Von Hagedorns'?

JOHN Does that mean I can get in or I can't get in? I haven't got that straight yet.

PARKER Can you get in?

JOHN Yeah, I told Dr. Von Hagedorn I can get house seats for any show on Broadway.

PARKER Go down there for a while, will you? Play with God-frey? I want to tell Ivy how well you're doing in school and your head is swollen enough as it is.
    (*A beat*)

JOHN Okay.
    (*He takes up his jacket*)

PARKER Say good-bye. Ivy can't stay long.

JOHN Good-bye . . .
    (*He kisses* IVY's *cheek; she kisses his*)

IVY Good-bye, my darling. It's been wonderful seeing you. This summer we're *definitely* going to spend a week at— Lake Whatever-it-is.
    (JOHN *starts upstage*)

PARKER Come back in time to dress.

JOHN Right.

IVY You're obliging, John; I like that.

JOHN   He beats me.
>   (JOHN *exits.* IVY *absorbs herself in her cottage cheese.*
>   *She wrinkles her nose*)

IVY   Ich! Whose cottage does this cheese come from; the Ancient Mariner's?
>   (*She inspects it closely*)

PARKER (*Rising*) There's a soda fountain on the corner that's famous for cottage cheese. Tell them I sent you.

IVY   Parker, please, hear me out. I don't pretend I've come here with unselfish motives. I'm lonely. I've made a life for myself and I'm sick of it. I want you back. I want you back more than I've ever wanted *anything,* and that includes to be an actress at age eight. It's true about Angela and Dion. Long after they were done with their rewriting they were spending whole nights together, in her room. They were overheard, not saying anything. You don't deserve that kind of dirty deal. I did a thousand rotten things to you, and I lash myself with each of them every day and every night, but I never did *that* rotten thing, and you know it.

PARKER (*Picking up her coat*) You'd better go now, Ivy. You'll feel better when you have a show set for next season.

IVY   I'm telling the truth, Parker.

PARKER (*Holding the coat open*) Angie will be here soon and I don't want her to see you.
>   (*A pause*)

IVY (*Putting aside the plate*) Okay, I'll go quietly. (*Rises, slips her arms into the coat*) You haven't said one word about my new coat.

PARKER I thought it was the old one turned sideways.

IVY (*Goes upstage, kisses her finger tips*) I still love you. I will always love you. Ancestors of mine have died in institutions.
(IVY *exits.* PARKER *closes the door, stays facing it.* CHARLOTTE *appears on the landing*)

CHARLOTTE How much do you believe?
(PARKER *turns, stares*)

PARKER (*Deeply shocked and offended*) Charlie . . . !

CHARLOTTE (*Coming down the stairs*) Well, you didn't think I *wouldn't* eavesdrop, did you? In my book any woman who looks *that* good in slacks is a bitch, period.

PARKER (*Coming downstage, shaking his head*) Boy . . .

CHARLOTTE Well, how much do you believe?

PARKER Only the last part, about the ancestors dying in institutions.
(*He sits*)

CHARLOTTE And the first part? Virtue dying in Boston?

PARKER Do you even have to ask, Charlie?

CHARLOTTE Yes, I do.

PARKER I don't believe a word of it. Not one syllable. You can relax.

CHARLOTTE That's what I expected. I, personally, think it's probably true.

PARKER *What?*

CHARLOTTE I do!

PARKER Charlie, you're—you're her mother!

CHARLOTTE Does that mean I have to be as naïve as her husband?

PARKER Naïve? I'm—I'm—

CHARLOTTE You're *naïve!* I *met* that Dion Kapakos last night; he's the youngest dirty old man I've ever seen! You leave Angela in his hands for three and a half of the most trying weeks in her life, you're free to visit her, but no, you sit right here on your fat integrity—how did you *think* they were going to wind up; bird-watching?
  (*She sits*)

PARKER You're—you're accusing your own daughter of infidelity!

CHARLOTTE I'm accusing her of nothing but being frightened and vulnerable and insecure and having a fool for a husband.

64

PARKER (*Rising*) I just don't understand you . . .

CHARLOTTE I told you before; I'm a lousy mother.
(PARKER *paces, stops*)

PARKER Ivy London, as a source of information, is about as reliable as a fortune cookie.
(*He paces again*)

CHARLOTTE (*Reminiscently*) I had a fortune cookie once that said, "A good name is better than precious oil." Next day, Esso dropped seven points. (*Picks up the plate of cottage cheese, sniffs it, grimaces*) You know, I could swear this stuff was absolutely fresh until she touched it.
(*She puts down the plate*)

PARKER (*Sitting*) No . . . I—I don't believe it. Not Angie. No.

CHARLOTTE Only an egotist could have such faith in his wife. Parker, last night at that theatre I saw Angela hanging on to Kapakos' hand as if he were the traffic cop at the school crossing. Pan that play tonight and it's ten to one you wake up tomorrow morning with more integrity and less wife than any man in town. Please don't risk it, Parker. You two are all I've got to brag about, now that I'm losing my figure.

PARKER God! Is there a woman somewhere who doesn't demand dishonesty of a man?

CHARLOTTE I've got news for you: honesty is *not* the most precious thing on earth; adding machines have honesty.

65

Love is the precious thing, and if you want it you have to give something for it, just as you have to give for anything else worth having. You've barricaded yourself with rules of what's right and wrong, what's honest and dishonest, and you're saying to Angela, "Obey all my rules; I'm not interested in any of yours." Well, that's not a husband talking, it's a tyrant; and the trouble with being a tyrant is that sooner or later comes the—Boston Tea Party.

(*A pause*)

PARKER I do not believe that Angie slept with Dion, and I do not believe that she'll run off with him if I review her play truthfully.

CHARLOTTE (*A long sigh*) All right, we'll change the subject. Let's talk about—geography. Tell me, Parker, how do you *know* the world is flat?

(ANGELA *enters through the front door; tired and subdued*)

ANGELA Hello.

CHARLOTTE Angela! We'd forgotten all about you! (PARKER *rises*) We've been sitting here talking about Agatha Christie. Parker is positive she has no staying power.

ANGELA (*In the foyer, removing her coat*) Hm?

PARKER Joke. How was the rehearsal?

ANGELA All right. Dion just wanted to keep everybody from sitting at home and worrying.

(*She hangs her coat in the closet*)

CHARLOTTE (*Sotto*) Well, he didn't quite succeed.

PARKER I made a dinner reservation for the four of us, at six-thirty.

ANGELA (*Coming downstage*) I'm sorry . . . I won't be able to make it . . . Dion's coming by at six; he's getting some gifts for the company; we want to give them out, and there are some other things he has to do at the theatre. (*Going to stairs and going up*) Besides, I couldn't eat anyway. I'm going to lie down for a while.

PARKER Butterflies in your stomach?

ANGELA Butterflies, bats, birds, bees . . .

CHARLOTTE There's a lifetime supply of telegrams on the dressing table.

ANGELA You ought to see the pile at the theatre. Sally sent a cable from Paris.

CHARLOTTE (*With unconcealed disgust*) I suppose *Marge* will send *flowers*.

PARKER Angie— (ANGELA, *about to exit into the bedroom, stops and turns back*) Angie, I—I've decided to break down and wear my dinner jacket for once.
   (*A beat*)

ANGELA For me? For little old worthless me? You're going to put on your great big painful dinner jacket, with the heavy lead collar and all those steel spikes in the lining?

67

Why, Ah declare, Mister Parker, you keep on this way, you're just goin' to spoil me rotten!
(*A beat.* JOHN *enters through front door, jacket slung over his shoulder*)

JOHN Hi.
(*A beat*)

ANGELA, PARKER *and* CHARLOTTE Hello.
(*Another beat.* PARKER *exits into the study.* ANGELA *exits into the bedroom.* CHARLOTTE *rises, takes the plate of cottage cheese, exits into the kitchen.* JOHN *looks around at the suddenly empty room*)

JOHN Oh boy. (*The lights fade to darkness. The telephone rings. A spot comes up on the telephone.* CHARLOTTE *answers it*)

CHARLOTTE Hello . . . Yes, she is, but I'd rather not disturb her unless it's urgent. Is there any message I could take? I'm her mother . . . Just a second. (*Finds pencil and paper, writes*) Francine Huskey . . . Is that H-U-S-K-E-Y? Oh, I-E. Right. And you're calling in reference to? (*Puts down pencil*) Passes for the show . . . Are you a friend of Angela's? Oh, I see. When was that? *Last* January? Oh, a *year ago* last January . . . And tell me, Miss Huskie, did you sit next to Angela for the *entire* train ride? . . . Just as far as Philadelphia . . . Well, Miss Huskie, I'm sure Angela will be delighted to send you free tickets. Any particular night? Saturday; of course . . . Are you sure one pair will be enough? Fine. Now just give me your address and we'll put the tickets right in the mail. Slowly now; I'm writing . . . (*With the phone tucked against her shoulder, she*

*begins methodically tearing to shreds the piece of paper
on which she wrote the name)* Mm-hmm . . . Mm-hmm
. . . Is there any apartment number? Mm-hmm. Oh, thank
you, Miss Huskie. And look, dear, for pity's sake don't be
selfish about this; I mean, if you should happen to run into
any of the *other* people who were on the train that day . . .
    *(The spot fades out. The doorbell rings. The lights come
    up. It is six o'clock and the spring sunlight is beginning
    to wane. The stage is empty. The doorbell rings again)*

PARKER *(Off, in bedroom)*   John, will you get it?

JOHN *(Off right, upstairs)*   Okay!
    *(*JOHN *enters, dressed as before; he starts downstairs)*

ANGELA *(Off, in bedroom)*   If it's Dion tell him I'll be down
in two minutes!
    *(*JOHN *goes upstage and opens the door. Sure enough, it
    is* DION*; in dinner clothes)*

DION *(Coming in as briskly as ever)*   Hiya, Johnny-boy! How
ya doin'?

JOHN *(Closing the door)*   Just great.

DION   Isn't Angie ready yet?

JOHN   She said she'll be down in two minutes.

DION *(At the foot of the stairs, calling up)*   Hey, Angie! I'm
double-parked!
    *(*JOHN *idles left toward the window)*

ANGELA (*Off, in bedroom*) I'll be as quick as I can!

JOHN (*Peering out through the curtains*) Oh boy, there's a cop . . .

DION (*Dashing left*) Where? Where? (JOHN *steps aside;* DION *looks anxiously through the window*) Where? Where?

JOHN At the police station.
(DION *turns, stares at* JOHN. JOHN *smiles, then crosses toward the stairs*)

DION You're a real funny kid, aren't you?

JOHN I get a yock once in a while.
(JOHN *starts up the stairs, then stops, as the bedroom door opens and* PARKER *emerges in dinner clothes*)

PARKER (*Into bedroom*) It's a *lovely* gown; I just said it's an unusual *color*, that's all.
(*He closes the door, and turns. He is facing toward* DION. *A beat*)

DION Hello.

PARKER Hello. (JOHN *resumes climbing the stairs as* PARKER *starts down*) You'd better get a move on; it's after six.

JOHN I know.
(JOHN *exits right.* PARKER *comes down, goes to the liquor cabinet near the study door, and takes out a glass*)

70

DION (*Moving to center*) That's a clever little fellow you've got there. How did you get him away from the Philip Morris people? (PARKER *throws him a glare, then pours whisky*) Thanks, I will. Straight Scotch. (PARKER *gets out another glass*) Do you always drink before an opening?

PARKER (*Pouring*) Only when I'm expecting a snake bite. (PARKER *holds out the drink;* DION *takes it*)

DION Thanks. Cheers.

PARKER (*Clearly, succinctly, and meaningfully*) Mud in your eye.
(*They drink*)

DION You know, you're an interesting guy, Parker. I've been doing some thinking about you.

PARKER Have you, now.

DION Ya . . . Have you ever been analyzed?

PARKER Not all of me; little specimens once or twice . . .

DION (*Smiling*) Not bad. But seriously, old man, look at the facts; you slammed Ivy London with a brutal review, didn't you?—and now you're all set to give Angie the very same treatment; it seems to me that you've got a pretty deep *hostility* toward the women you marry.

PARKER Do I get to look at some ink blots, or is that it?

DION Oh, come on now, don't get defensive. I'm in analysis myself, and it's done me a hell of a lot of good. Man, I was aggressive, destructive, a compulsive braggart, self, self, self, that's all I ever thought about.

PARKER   That was *before* analysis? (*ANGELA enters from the bedroom, looking smashingly beautiful even if her gown is an unusual color. She carries a purse and a fur stole. DION rises, puts down his drink, and moves to the foot of stairs. PARKER drifts to center stage*) Well, she's *prettier* than Tennessee Williams anyway.

DION   (*To ANGELA, as she descends the stairs*) Prettier than anyone on earth.

ANGELA   Thank you. Did you get the gifts?

DION   They're in the car. I got cuff links for the men, earrings for the women, and one of each for the rest of the cast.
(*DION smiles, ANGELA smiles, PARKER ignores them; sips his drink. DION takes ANGELA's stole, holds it for her*)

ANGELA   (*Refusing it, eyes on PARKER*)   No, not yet, Dion.

DION   Angie, I'm—

ANGELA   You're double-parked; I know. But we'll have to stay for another minute or two. I have to speak to Parker. (*PARKER turns to face ANGELA. A beat. DION puts the stole on a chair. ANGELA's eyes are still on PARKER*) What time is it?

DION   (*Glancing at his watch*)   Ten after six.

72

ANGELA   All right . . . Are you still planning to cover the show?
   (*A beat*)

PARKER   You know I am.

ANGELA   I don't want you to. I want you to call the paper and let Harvey Rittenhouse cover it.

PARKER   Harvey Rittenhouse is a blob.
   (*A beat*)

ANGELA   (*Great tension*)   I don't want you to review my play.

PARKER   I'm sorry, Angie. I'm going to.
   (*A beat*)

ANGELA   All right . . . I have a list here . . . (*Opening her purse, showing a folded sheet of paper*) A list of some of the things you've said about the play . . . Things like— calling it a Hupmobile, and saying it would decay teeth . . . When you sit down in that aisle seat tonight, I'm hand- ing this list to Sid Champlain. I've spoken to him about this situation, and he feels that a critic has no right coming into a theatre as prejudiced as you are about *A Houseful of Silence*. If you review it, no matter what kind of review you write, he's going to complain—and complain *loudly*—to the League of New York Theatres, and the paper, and whoever else will be interested in hearing him. He's going to make trouble for you, all the trouble he can. You're not the most well-liked critic, you know.
   (*She pushes the list back into her purse, closes it. A pause*)

PARKER Angie, you're under a terrific strain and you're say-ing things—

ANGELA (*On "and"*) Don't you make excuses for me! I know exactly what I'm doing!

PARKER Then you ought to have your face slapped. You're talking to your husband.

ANGELA No, I'm not! That's something else you said; on open-ing night you're a critic and I'm a playwright, and I'm not your wife. Then you're not my husband either.

DION (*Moving closer to* ANGELA's *side*) You *did* say that, Parker. I was standing right here.

ANGELA It's after six. It's opening night. I'm a playwright and you're a critic; that's all. And I'm not going to let you come gunning for me with the kind of black-box review you've been dreaming up ever since I began the play! Well? Do I give the list to Champlain?

PARKER Is that when you stopped being my wife; at six o'clock?
  (*A beat*)

ANGELA When did you stop being my husband?
  (*A beat*)

PARKER Ivy was here this afternoon. She says there was gossip in Boston about you two.

DION You know gossip, old man. Especially in Boston. I mean, what the hell else is there to do *but* gossip?

PARKER   She said he was in your room, all night . . .

ANGELA   (*Coolly*)   It's after six o'clock. Since when does a critic ask questions about a playwright's personal affairs?

PARKER   Don't play games with me, Angie.

ANGELA   I'm not playing games. You think you can—throw away *one* half of me and still cross-examine the other half? I am *one person* and you disowned me and it's a little bit late to start wondering if anything happened in my room! *You should have been there!*

PARKER   You know why I stayed away.

ANGELA   (*Her hurt showing again*)   No I don't! I don't know anything! All I know is you lied for Ivy *six times,* and for me you won't even just keep quiet! Well, *Dion* feels differently about me! *Dion* was with me, believing in me and helping me, treating me as an equal, as an adult, not patronizing me and making fun of me! (*Pointing at* DION) *Dion* happens to love me!

   (PARKER *stares at* DION, *who would rather be anywhere else on earth*)

DION   (*Squirms*)   Well, I *do* . . .

PARKER   (*Venomously*)   You're double-parked.

ANGELA   Oh, no! No, he isn't! Not tonight. Tonight, I don't have a husband. You made the rules, not I. Now, tell me something, when does opening night end? At midnight, at two, at six in the morning? When? Because there's a party

tonight after the show and Dion's taking me, and I'd like to know where I stand, and how much I should drink and when I should leave and whose house I should go home to! (PARKER *stares at her, wordless*) Well?
  (*She waits another moment, then snatches her stole from* DION *and starts for the door.* DION *follows*)

PARKER Angie! (*She stops and turns.* PARKER *takes a ticket envelope from his pocket, shows it, drops it on the table*) You win. Leave them at the box office in Harvey's name. I'll call the paper. (*A beat.* ANGELA *is suddenly uncertain, dismayed. She comes downstage and hesitantly takes the envelope*) One of those tickets was for John.

ANGELA (*Putting the envelope into her purse and taking out two tickets*) I have *two* tickets, for you *and* for John. Next to the single that Mom has. (*An uncomfortable beat*) Will you get the elevator, Dion?

DION Right.
  (*He exits*)

PARKER Just leave one of them. I'm not going.
  (*A beat*)

ANGELA All right. (*Putting one ticket on the table, returning the other one to her purse*) If that's the way you want it . . .
  (*She starts upstage*)

PARKER It isn't. Nothing is the way I want it.
  (ANGELA *stops at the door, and turns*)

76

ANGELA You should have loved me enough to *say* the play was good, even if it isn't.

PARKER No. No, that's not love.

ANGELA Says who?
    (*She exits.* PARKER *stands for a moment, then picks up his glass, crosses to the liquor cabinet and pours another drink*)

CHARLOTTE (*Off right, upstairs*) Angela? (*Enters on the landing, and goes to the bedroom door*) Angela?
    (*She opens the door*)

PARKER She's gone.

CHARLOTTE (*Turning*) Why didn't she wait? I wanted to give her a speech about fortitude in the face of adversity. (PARKER *drinks.* CHARLOTTE *starts down the stairs. She is wearing an evening gown and a matching coat, and she carries a purse*) Don't just stand there; compliment me.

PARKER You look swell.

CHARLOTTE Thanks. I feel like Marie Antoinette, all dressed up for the guillotine.

PARKER That ticket there is for John. Take it. I'm not going.
    (*A beat*)

CHARLOTTE Not going at all?

PARKER That's right.

CHARLOTTE Well ... (*Going to the table, taking the ticket*) What finally got through that thick head of yours?
(*She puts the ticket into her purse*)

PARKER Just one of those steel balls they use to demolish buildings.
(*He drinks.* CHARLOTTE *looks at him with concern*)

CHARLOTTE Parker—

PARKER Do you have money for dinner?
(JOHN *enters on the landing, wearing his best blue suit. He stops*)

CHARLOTTE No.

PARKER (*Taking out his wallet*) I made a reservation at a place right across from the theatre. Chateau something ...
(*He takes bills from the wallet*)

JOHN Aren't you having dinner with us?
(*A beat.* PARKER *doesn't turn*)

PARKER No, I'm not.
(*He gives the bills to* CHARLOTTE)

CHARLOTTE He isn't feeling well.

JOHN (*Coming down a few steps*) You're going to meet us at the theatre?
(*A beat*)

PARKER No. I'm not going to the theatre. Charlie has a ticket for you.

78

JOHN (*Coming farther down*) That's crazy . . . You went when you had the fractured hip, didn't you?

PARKER I don't feel well and I'm not going, that's all.
(*He drinks*)

JOHN Who's going to cover the show?

PARKER All the other critics. Don't worry; justice will be done.

JOHN Who's going to cover it for *our* paper?

PARKER I don't know . . .

JOHN Harvey Rittenhouse?

PARKER (*Busying himself with more whisky-pouring*) Probably . . .

CHARLOTTE (*Moving to the foyer*) Come on, John; you're stuck with me; resign yourself.

JOHN (*Not hearing her, facing* PARKER'S *back*) Why aren't you going?

PARKER (*Turning to him*) Because I'm not feeling well! Now go on with Charlie!

JOHN You said as long as you were living you would never let Harvey Rittenhouse—

PARKER (*On "let"*) *I'm not going because Angie doesn't want me to! Now will you get out of here?* It's six-thirty, almost . . .

JOHN You said sometimes you had to hurt people . . .

PARKER Charlie—
(*He puts down the glass*)

JOHN You said you would hurt them more if you lost your self-respect!

PARKER (*Over the above*) Charlie, will you get him out of here?
(CHARLOTTE *comes downstage*)

JOHN (*Continuing without a break*) That was the most important thing you ever told me, all that about self-respect!

PARKER I was wrong! I changed my mind!

CHARLOTTE (*Taking* JOHN's *arm*) John—

JOHN You said you would never sell a—

PARKER (*On "would"*) *Will you stop telling me what I said? You're like that damn recording machine in there!* Go on. It's late.

CHARLOTTE (*Trying to draw* JOHN *away*) John . . .
(JOHN *won't move. A beat*)

JOHN Come on to the theatre!

PARKER Holy—!
(PARKER's *hand comes up, then he ducks into the study, slams the door, leans against it.* JOHN *pulls away from* CHARLOTTE, *rushes to the study door and begins kicking it again and again.* PARKER *claps a hand over his eyes.* CHARLOTTE *pulls* JOHN *away from the door*)

CHARLOTTE Stop it! John!   JOHN Let go of me! Let me
John—now stop! Stop!   go! I'll kick him! I'll kick
                               that door! Let go of me!
(PARKER *opens the door. He musters his last vestige of
authority*)

PARKER Now you listen to me, John. You go with Charlotte
and you go to dinner and you go to the theatre, or so help
me God I'll give you a whaling that you'll—never forget as
long as you live (*A pause.* CHARLOTTE *releases* JOHN. *He
stands angrily*) Now do as I tell you.
(*A beat*)

JOHN I don't care if you *don't* go to the theatre. I don't care
if you never go any place. I don't care if you get inside there
and lock the door and stay there until you're dead.
(*He turns, walks upstage and exits*)

CHARLOTTE Parker . . .

PARKER Stay with him . . . (CHARLOTTE *hurries upstage and
exits.* PARKER *wipes a hand over his face. After a moment he
takes his glass from the liquor cabinet, and drinks. A pause.
He looks at the phone, goes to it. A beat. He puts down the
glass, picks up the receiver, dials a number, picks up the
glass, drinks. The sun is gone now; a dusky blueness has
infiltrated the room, and grows deeper until curtain*) Exten-
sion eighty-three . . . Leonard? Parker. Is Lee there? . . .
Well, leave a note for him, will you? Tell him that I'm not
covering the opening tonight. The tickets are at the box
office in Harvey's name . . . Personal reasons . . . Yes. Now
look, don't *you* start telling me what I said! . . . How
should I know where Harvey is? Try the Laffmovie on

Forty-second Street! (*He hangs up, goes to the liquor cabinet, refuels, drinks. A pause. He goes to the couch, takes the
phone, sits on the couch, pulling the phone down beside him.
One-handed, he lifts the receiver and dials the operator*)
Western Union, please . . . Gramercy 7-3935. (*Drinks*) I'd
like to send a telegram, please . . . Angela Ballantine . . .
Ballantine. B as in beer, A as in ale, L as in lager—that's
right; Ballantine. Forty-fourth Street Theatre, East of Broadway, New York. This is to be delivered immediately. (*During this he stretches out full-length on the couch, with the
phone sitting on his chest*) "Congratulations . . . on the
opening . . . of your first play. Certain it will be . . . a
huge success . . . bringing you fame . . . fortune . . . and
deep and enduring personal happiness." That's signed "Lillian Hellman and Clare Boothe Luce" . . . Gramercy
7-3935; Parker Ballantine. (*He hangs up, drinks, thinks,
puts down the glass, looks at the phone, lifts the receiver,
hesitates, slowly dials a number. A pause*) Ivy? . . . You're
a rat. And a louse. And several other small animals . . .
Sure she denied it! Sort of . . . You're a rat; I just wanted
to get it on the record . . . I *am* miserable. I'm kindly old
Uncle Ben, all alone in the gathering twilight, hanging out
the old placard, "Rooms For Rent." In the Greek version
I shoot myself . . . No, it's just a joke. . . . Hey, Ivy, what
are you doing? . . Come on over, will you? Say funny
things and rub my back for me? . . . Oh, Florence Night-
ingale is smiling down upon you . . . Run, do not walk
. . . Hey, Ivy, Ivy-Rat, hey . . . I've been thinking it over
about your Helen of Troy . . . It was a *beautiful* perform-
ance, Ivy, just *beautiful* . . .

The Curtain Falls

ACT THREE

ACT THREE

The blinds have been drawn beneath the window curtains, and several lamps have been lighted. PARKER *is still supine on the couch, his back against its arm and his feet up. His shoes are on the floor, his dinner jacket is draped over a nearby chair, the telephone is back where it belongs, and the Scotch bottle is near at hand.* PARKER *takes it up and refills his glass.*

PARKER   I want to drink; I don't want to eat!
  (IVY *enters from the kitchen with a tablecloth*)

IVY   Just come drink at the table for a while; it *looks* nicer.

PARKER   No. Appearances count for nothing with us alcoholics.
  (*During the following,* IVY *removes whatever is on the dining table and spreads the cloth. She is wearing another slack suit, or maybe these are lounging pajamas. Anyway, they're bright red and interesting to watch. She has on a postage stamp apron as well*)

IVY   To think I would see the day when my old Parker would refuse a dish of Beef Stroganoff.

PARKER   (*Raising himself*)   Beef Stroganoff?

IVY   Mm-hmm.

PARKER   You're kidding.

85

IVY Scout's honor.

PARKER (*Dropping back*) Ah, you can't even boil an egg; where did you learn to make Beef Stroganoff?

IVY In the cab, on the way over here. "Place container in four-hundred-and-fifty degree oven for thirty minutes. Remove cover and serve." God bless America.
(*She exits into the kitchen*)

PARKER (*Calling after her*) All right, if it's Beef Stroganoff I'll eat. We'll just put a little Scotch in it, that's all. (*Looks at his watch, listens to it*) What time is it?

IVY (*Off*) Twenty-five of eight.

PARKER (*Removing the watch*) What?

IVY (*Entering with plates, silverware and napkins*) Twenty-five of eight.
(*During the following,* IVY *sets the table for two*)

PARKER (*Setting the watch, then winding it*) Eight o'clock the curtain goes up . . .

IVY Revealing onstage an egg the size of a zeppelin.

PARKER (*Drinks*) At this moment, backstage at the Forty-fourth Street Theatre, Dion Kapakos, boy louse, is feeding pep and optimism to his hardy band of tomorrow's unemployed . . . while Angie flits from dressing room to dressing room, distributing earrings and cuff links; pennies on the eyelids of a corpse. And down the street comes the rat-

like figure of Harvey Rittenhouse, his tiny nose twitching with uncontrollable glee. What joy for Harvey to enter a theatre that is neither church basement nor converted bordello!
(He winds his watch some more)

IVY Does the knife go on the right or the left?

PARKER In my back, baby, in my back.

IVY One-potato, two-potato, three-potato, four; five-potato, six-potato, seven-potato, more.
(She places the knife)

PARKER *(Shakes the watch, listens)* I broke the spring . . . Symbolism . . . I cannot stand symbolism!
(He hurls the watch across the room)

IVY Parker!

PARKER Don't worry, it's just the old watch my father gave me on his deathbed . . . (IVY *retrieves the watch, inspects it, puts it someplace*) That worm Kapakos . . . I was supposed to be *his* father. "You're a *father image* for me," he said.

IVY *(Returning to the table)* Well, he *is* Greek, you know. Oedipus, and all that.

PARKER Now I'm nobody's father image. John despises me.

IVY *(Finished with table setting)* He'll get over it. What do you want on your salad?

PARKER Scotch. (IVY *exits into kitchen.* PARKER *lies there for a moment, then addresses an unseen inquisitor*) You ask me, sir, how I, a man of evident breeding and intellect, come to be lying here in this Bowery doorway . . . I shall tell you. When I was a youth in the small town of Innocence, Nebraska, there chanced to fall into my hands a volume, bound in green buckram; the critical essays of Max Beerbohm. I read the volume once, twice, three times; ambition flamed in my bosom; I, too, would be a drama critic! Tying together all my belongings in a polka-dot kerchief, I bade adieu to my kindly old parents and set forth on foot for New York City. When at last I reached the sprawling metropolis, I sought employment at the offices of its leading journal, and there, in the humble capacity of copy boy, I won the friendship of the kindly old drama critic, Sage Arbiter. He taught me all he knew, and then some. One day Destiny pointed its finger; my kindly old mentor fell victim to a tainted halibut. "Catastrophe!" cried the editor. "Who shall cover tonight's opening of the revival of Henrik Ibsen's immortal *The Wild Duck?*" Ah, you have guessed it! Yes, it was I who ran with heart thumping to the glittering theatre and sat on the edge of the critic's aisle seat. The production was a disaster. I returned to the paper and wrote my first review. "If this is *The Wild Duck,*" I said, "then I'll just have the vegetable plate." Sixteen years later I was at the top of my profession. No symposium on the state of the theatre was complete without my expressions of asinine optimism. I had a son who worshiped me, and a wife who adored me. The world was my oyster, and each day a pearl. And then, one morning, my wife turned to me, and smiled, and said, "Darling, I have an idea . . ." (*Reaching out*) Please, sir, thirty cents for a bottle of muscatel . . .

(IVY *enters with two bowls of salad. She places them on the table, steps back and surveys her handiwork*)

IVY That looks right, doesn't it?

PARKER What time is it?

IVY Now look, this is a woman's wrist watch; if I have to read it more than once in an hour I go blind. It's seventeen minutes of eight, and that's the last report you get. (*Draws out a chair right of the table, sits*) Whew! I'm exhausted.
(*She fans herself*)

PARKER (*Patting couch beside him*) Come here.
(*A beat.* IVY *rises, removes apron, puts it over the center chair, goes to the couch and sits where* PARKER *patted. He draws her down. They kiss, lengthily and thoroughly*)

IVY I tell you, they don't kiss like that any more . . .

PARKER You say we've got thirty whole minutes before that Stroganoff is done?
(*He draws her down; they kiss again. Then they look at each other*)

IVY No, we're going to eat. *Then* we'll pour some black coffee into you, and *then* we'll go over to my place. And we'll leave the dishes for Angela.

PARKER Your place?

IVY Mm-hmm.
(*She takes* PARKER's *glass, sips*)

PARKER No . . . you don't want me now . . .

IVY Oh, don't I! Ha! I'm not letting you out of my sight from here on in. That's a blood oath.
    (*She sips*)

PARKER I'm just a husk of a man . . .

IVY Ah, my poor baby, she really hurt you, didn't she . . . (PARKER *nods;* IVY *feeds him some Scotch*) It never fails; the girls who wear those flouncy little dirndls are bitches, every one of them.

PARKER No, no, not Angie. No, she isn't . . .

IVY Taking your tickets from you? Locking you out of the theatre? Who does she think she is, the *Shuberts* or something? Oh, Parker, you were right to pan my Helen of Troy! You were! I can face that now! It *was* Troy, New York! It was! (*They kiss passionately*) I love you with all my heart!

PARKER (*Kisses* IVY *lightly, pats her cheek*) You said you would rub my back for me . . .

IVY Oh, yes! Yes! Turn over, darling!

PARKER (*Turning over*) Easy now; I'm a wounded veteran . . . (IVY *begins massaging his back. He reaches out*) Buy a poppy, sir?

IVY (*Soothingly rubbing*) Aaaaaahhhhhhh . . .

90

PARKER Mmmmmmmmmmmmmm . . . She's not a *bitch,* but you know, she's not exactly a woolly lamb either.

IVY I'll say she's not! Look what she's done to you. Pulverized you.

PARKER Higher. Mmmmmmmm . . .

IVY What kind of life can you have with her now? Can you ever stand up to her again, put her in her place?

PARKER No, I can't . . . I guess I can't . . . Not after tonight.

IVY She's trampled on you! I loathe her!

PARKER *Ow!*

IVY Oh, I'm sorry, darling, I'm sorry! (*Kisses the back of* PARKER's *neck, rubs it tenderly*) Aaaahhhh . . .
    (*A pause*)

PARKER Those weren't my *tickets* I gave her . . . They were something *infinitely more precious* than my tickets!
    (*He would rise, but* IVY's *massaging pushes him down*)

IVY That's right! And she *took* them from you!

PARKER And now Harvey Rittenhouse has them!
    (*Again he would rise; again* IVY *holds him down*)

IVY She's finished the marriage completely! It's done! Kaput!

PARKER It is . . . (*Interrupting massage, turning and sitting up*) It's true . . . It is . . . kaput. Everything. Angie, John, me . . . (*Rubs his forehead woozily*) I said I wouldn't sell out, and she scared me, and I *did* sell out, and everything's . . . kaput . . . finished . . .

IVY (*Throwing her arms around him*) I'm *glad* she's done it, my darling! I'll make things right for you! And for John too! I'm a new Ivy, you'll see I am! Oh, Parker-Love—
    (*She tries to kiss him; he fends her off clumsily*)

PARKER Ivy . . . Ivy . . . I've got to get to that theatre . . .

IVY What?

PARKER I've got to get to that theatre, and see the show, and beat Harvey back to the office and *write my review!*
    (*He tries to get to his feet;* IVY *pulls him down*)

IVY You can't go to the theatre! It's too late! It's, it's—oh, damn this watch!
    (*She turns away toward the light, and squints at her watch.* PARKER *rises unsteadily*)

PARKER Have to . . . Have to risk her leaving . . .

IVY (*Catching his arm*) It's ten of eight! It's too late!

PARKER Curtain won't go up till ten after. It never does; they announce it for eight, it goes up at ten after. They're liars, all of them . . . (*Pulls his arm free and starts for his dinner jacket in gluey slow-motion*) Got twenty minutes . . . Cab up Eighth Avenue, cut across Forty-fourth. Make it in plenty of time . . .

IVY You're drunk, Parker!

PARKER Ten more drinks and I'd still be a better critic than Harvey Rittenhouse ... (*Starts getting into his dinner jacket; it's not easy*) Have to risk her leaving ... No chance for anything if I stay here ...

IVY (*Rising*) You can't go to the theatre in this condition! You're pie-eyed!

PARKER (*Draws himself up; suddenly authoritative*) Actors can act when they're drunk, can't they? Playwrights can playwrite when they're drunk. Well, damn it, I say a critic can critic when he's drunk! (*Lapsing back into booziness*) Shoes ... Must wear shoes ... Never go to the theatre without shoes ...
    (*He starts back toward the couch.* IVY *snatches up his shoes and clutches them to her bosom*)

IVY I won't let you do this! I won't! Come to *my* place, Parker! Let her have her little victory!
    (*A beat*)

PARKER (*Pointing an icy finger*) Ivy ... you give me those shoes ... or I will dissect you, and put you in suitcases, and ship you to New Haven and Boston and Philadelphia and Washington.
    (IVY *gives him the shoes. He sits on the couch, and laboriously puts them on*)

IVY You don't have a ticket! How will you get into the theatre?

PARKER Buy one from somebody. Ten dollars, twenty dollars; mezzanine, balcony . . . (*Looks up, chuckles*) Ha, ha . . . Somebody's gonna get twenty dollars for a balcony seat for *Houseful of Silence!* Ha, ha . . .
(*He is back to the shoes*)

IVY I'm going with you! I'm not letting you out of my sight!
(*She runs upstage, gets her coat from the closet*)

PARKER Shoelaces are unnecessary . . .
(*He rises and weaves toward the study.* IVY *comes downstage, putting on her coat*)

IVY Review the play! Good! Go ahead! You'll blow the marriage into tiny pieces! Good! The sooner the better!

PARKER (*Going into study*) Cross that bridge when I come to it . . . Can't let everything be ruined without putting up a fight . . . (*He takes his black box from the shelf, returns to the living room, puts the box on the table and begins transferring its hundred slips of paper by fistfuls into his trouser pockets, side jacket pockets, breast pocket, every pocket.* IVY *watches fearfully, her hand over her mouth.* PARKER *mutters on as he arms himself*) Thinks because she's a playwright I have to stop being a critic . . . Thinks she can scare me into giving my tickets to Harvey Rittenhouse . . . Thinks I'm afraid of Dion Kapakos and Oedipus and S. P. Champlain and the League of New York Theatres . . . (*Turns emptied box upside down, shakes it, drops it on floor. Points to the door*) To Forty-fourth Street!
(*He starts upstage*)

IVY Parker! For God's sake, stop! Look at yourself! *People will see you!*

(PARKER *stops, turns, stands undulating for a moment. He touches his rumpled hair, his undone tie, his pockets that are stuffed and brimming with bits of paper. He smiles innocently*)

PARKER They won't believe it's me.
(*And out he goes, calling "Taxi! Taxi!" with* IVY *despairingly following and slamming the door as the lights fade. When the lights come up, everything is as before. The front door opens.* CHARLOTTE *enters, followed by* JOHN. CHARLOTTE *comes downstage, putting the keys in her purse and the purse on the table.* JOHN *stays sullenly in the doorway*)

CHARLOTTE Lordy! Never in my life have I attended a party where there was less to drink and more to get drunk about . . . Parker? (*Looks into study, then glances around the room and up at the closed bedroom door*) Come in, John; nobody's going to bite you. (JOHN *steps forward, closes the door, stays upstage.* CHARLOTTE *removes her gloves*) You were my savior, darling. An older escort, and I would have had to stick it out until the reviews came in. I'd have wound up like S. P. Champlain. Did you see him, sitting there eating his handkerchief?

JOHN The review on television wasn't so bad.

CHARLOTTE "Periods of tedium" is not a complimentary phrase, John. Not even in television. (*Removing coat*) "Periods of tedium"; ha! If you ask me, the only period of un-tedium was two minutes after the curtain went up, when that old woman in the balcony started shouting about people coming in late and drunk and stepping on her toes. (*Puts

95

her coat on a chair) Now you can't stand there all night. Go up and apologize to your father. Tell him you're sorry you said those unkind things.

JOHN Something smells.

CHARLOTTE Don't be nasty.

JOHN I'm not being nasty; something *smells*. In there.
(*He indicates the kitchen*)

CHARLOTTE (*Sniffs*) You're right . . . (*She crosses quickly and exits into kitchen. A beat.* JOHN *comes downstage, stands before the opened study door, closes it. A beat.* CHARLOTTE *comes out of the kitchen, bearing, on a pot holder, an aluminum container. Within it is a hardened black residue which she prods with a spoon*) Your father doesn't resole his own galoshes, does he?

JOHN The table is set for two people . . .

CHARLOTTE (*Putting the pot holder and container on dining table*) Yes . . . And somebody's been wearing Angela's party apron . . . (*She fingers it*)

JOHN And somebody's been sitting in my chair.
(*A beat.* CHARLOTTE *looks up at the bedroom door, puts a hand on* JOHN's *shoulder*)

CHARLOTTE You stay here . . . (*Crosses, goes quickly upstairs, taps softly at the bedroom door*) Parker? (*Taps again, then opens the door*) Parker? (*She peers in, opens the door wide, steps back*)

96

JOHN   Isn't he there?

CHARLOTTE   (*Looks off right, cranes her neck, shrugs*)   No
Papa Bear, no Goldilocks, no nobody.
   (*She starts downstairs*)

JOHN   The black box . . . (*Goes to it, picks it up*) It's empty.
Do you think someone broke in?

CHARLOTTE   Who; a band of daring young playwrights? (*She
goes to the couch, picks up a whisky glass, rubs its edge*)

JOHN   (*Putting down the box*)   Lipstick?

CHARLOTTE   All right, you can go to sleep, Doctor Watson;
I'll handle this case myself.

JOHN   Angie said I can play hooky tomorrow.

CHARLOTTE   You still need some sleep. It's nearly one o'clock.
   (ANGELA, *armed with a folded newspaper, flings open
   the front door like Carry Nation raiding a saloon.* DION
   is behind her, several other newspapers under his arm)

ANGELA   Where is he?

CHARLOTTE   Parker?

JOHN   Are those the reviews?

ANGELA   (*Coming in*)   Where is he? Hiding away in the bedroom?
   (DION *follows her in, closes the door*)

97

CHARLOTTE He's not here, darling. He's out. I don't know where.

JOHN Are those the reviews?

ANGELA (*Brandishing the newspaper*) He reviewed the play!
      (*A beat*)

CHARLOTTE (*Softly*) What . . . ?

DION He slashed it.
      (*A beat*)

JOHN Dad . . . reviewed the play . . . ?

CHARLOTTE But we saw that—that what's-his-name—Rittenhouse, sitting there, smiling, nodding . . .

ANGELA (*Showing* CHARLOTTE, *pointing*) *Parker wrote the review!*

JOHN He was . . . at the theatre . . . ?

ANGELA Yes, he was at the theatre! Somewhere, somehow . . .
      (*She hurls the folded paper to the couch*)

DION The other reviews aren't very good, but his is the crusher. We'll be lucky if we last till Saturday.

JOHN (*Takes up the newspaper; slowly, with both hands, reverently*) " 'Opening Night Report,' by Parker Ballantine" . . . !

DION How does it feel, being the Son of Dracula?
(ANGELA *puts a restraining hand on* DION's *arm.* JOHN, *reading raptly, moves left*)

ANGELA They're in the closet, Dion. On the shelf. Just the small one.

DION Right.
(DION *puts the newspapers aside, goes upstage to the foyer closet.* ANGELA *slips off her stole*)

CHARLOTTE Just the small what?

ANGELA The small suitcase.
(*She puts down the stole*)

JOHN (*As he reads, with delectation*) Ooohhh . . . !

CHARLOTTE Angela . . .

ANGELA (*Keeping herself forcibly under control*) I'll only take a few things tonight. Tomorrow I want you to pack everything else. I'll tell you where to send it.

CHARLOTTE Angela—

ANGELA Don't advise me, Mother! Please. He *knew* how I felt. I told him! And he gave me his tickets! (*To* DION) Upstairs . . .
(DION *crosses with the suitcase, and starts upstairs.* ANGELA *would follow, but* CHARLOTTE *catches her arm*)

CHARLOTTE Listen to me, Angela!

ANGELA No! No, Mother, I'm not listening to anyone! Not any more! I'm listening to *me* for a change. This is *my* life and I'm taking charge of it! I'm going to do what I want to do, and be what I want to be, and I don't care if I never—

CHARLOTTE (*On "care"*) This is no time to recite "Invictus"!
(ANGELA *pulls free and starts upstairs as* DION *exits into the bedroom.* CHARLOTTE *looks around helplessly*)

JOHN (*With greater delectation*) Ooooooooohhhhh . . . !

CHARLOTTE Oh, Lord . . .
(*She starts up the stairs after* ANGELA)

ANGELA (*Nearing the bedroom door*) There's a gray suit in the closet, Dion, and those shoes under the dressing table, and—

CHARLOTTE (*Catching* ANGELA *in the doorway, pulling her back*) You stay out here for a minute!

ANGELA Mother—!

CHARLOTTE (*A desperate whisper*) You're crazy! Insane! You can't go flying off to Never-Neverland with that Peter Pan in there!

ANGELA I don't know! I don't know *where* I'm going or with whom! But I can't stay here, Mama! I can't! Read that review! He's a bully and a sadist and an egomaniac and—and—

CHARLOTTE And he's pompous and self-righteous and he takes his work too seriously and you love him!

CRITIC'S CHOICE

ANGELA   No! I hate him! I never want to see him again, not if I live to be five thousand!
   (*She exits into the bedroom, slams the door*)

CHARLOTTE   (*Turning*)   Oh, dear God, there goes my last daughter!
   (*She leans wearily against the landing rail. A pause. JOHN, finished reading, looks up*)

JOHN   You want to hear it?
   (*A beat*)

CHARLOTTE   All right . . . Give it to me slowly. One barrel at a time . . .
   (*As JOHN reads the review, CHARLOTTE comes down the stairs; weakly, holding the banister*)

JOHN   (*Taking center stage and reading with pride*)   " 'Opening Night Report,' by Parker Ballantine. I think it's time for all us Transylvanian peasants to pick up our torches and march menacingly up to that castle on the hill, because Dr. Frankenstein is making monsters again. (CHARLOTTE *groans. She sits on the sofa and does quite a bit of groaning throughout the following*) This time he's attached the arms and legs of Agamemnon to the torso of Rebecca of Sunnybrook Farm. S. P. Champlain has led the creature over to the Forty-fourth Street Theatre, where last night it stumbled around for a few minutes, grunted, and fell over dead. (ANGELA *and* DION *emerge from the bedroom;* ANGELA *with a light coat over her shoulders and carrying a small cosmetics case;* DION *carrying the suitcase. They start downstairs*) Just for the record, *A Houseful of Silence* was written by Angela Ballantine, directed by Dion Kapakos, and produced by mistake. (*The front door opens.* PARKER *enters, rumpled but sober.* IVY *is with him.* ANGELA *has just reached the foot of the stairs,* DION *behind her.* ANGELA *and* PARKER *confront each other as* JOHN, *unaware of* PARKER's *entrance, continues reading*) Several actors were involved. The only thing they can do now is change their names and start over. Okay, men, light the torches! A cleaner Transylvania is up to us!"

PARKER It's short, but I think it makes its point.

JOHN (*Drops paper on coffee table, runs upstage to* PARKER) Dad! Boy! Boy—! Those were *all new* ones!

PARKER (*Grins, takes* JOHN's *shoulders, meets* ANGELA's *eyes again*) I've already had my last meal. Do I get a cigarette before you shoot?

ANGELA I'm not shooting, Parker. I'm leaving.

DION With me.

ANGELA I've decided not to give Sid Champlain that list of your prejudiced witticisms. I'm not interested in taking petty revenge on you; I'm interested only in getting out.

JOHN Don't go, Angie . . .

ANGELA I'm sorry, John. When you're older you'll know more about the man-woman relationship and you'll understand why I'm doing this.

PARKER You'll know *less* about the man-woman relationship; believe me, you'll know less.

ANGELA I see *you* don't have any qualms about changing horses in midstream.

IVY (*On* PARKER's *arm again*) Smile when you say that, darling.

PARKER Ivy came here to bandage the wounds that *you* inflicted on me. (*Freeing his arm and taking* IVY's *hand*) You've done a fine job, Ivy. Good nurse. Bless you.

IVY I'm not going.

DION "Dracula Meets the Spider Lady."

IVY Dion . . . *dear* Dion . . . isn't it time you returned that tuxedo?
　　(*She slips off her coat*)

ANGELA (*Taking up the cosmetics case*) Let's go, Dion.

PARKER Hold on a minute.

ANGELA For what? A lecture?
　　(DION *moves up beside* ANGELA, *with the suitcase*)

PARKER A small speech.

ANGELA No, thanks.

PARKER You keep asking to be treated like an adult; then act like one. Stop running. You're not fifteen any more. (*A beat.* ANGELA *stands frozen.* CHARLOTTE, *behind* DION, *gently detaches the suitcase from his hand, sets it on floor, smiles sweetly at him.* PARKER *crouches down before* JOHN) John, I'd like you to do a favor for me.

JOHN What?

PARKER I'd like you to go upstairs and get into your pajamas and get into bed. Everything's going to be all right.

ANGELA Huh!

JOHN (*Looks at* ANGELA, *then at* PARKER *again*) How can it be?

PARKER It will be. Trust me.
(*A beat*)

JOHN Okay.

PARKER (*Stands straight*) I thank you, sir . . .
(JOHN *goes to the stairs, putting down the newspaper en route. He starts up*)

JOHN One of these days there's going to be a big scene and I'm not going to have to go offstage for it . . .
(*He exits right.* PARKER *moves downstage*)

CHARLOTTE (*Sitting on the couch*) I'm staying. *Somebody* has to represent the stockholders.

ANGELA All right, let's have the speech.

PARKER It would help if you would put down your luggage.
(*A beat*)

ANGELA (*Accepting the challenge*) All right.
(*She puts down stole and cosmetics case, comes downstage.* DION *touches her hand as she passes*)

PARKER First of all, I have a couple of apologies to make to
you.

IVY Apologies? *You're* going to apologize to *her?*

PARKER (*Over the "to her?"*) Shut up, Ivy. (*To* ANGELA)
When you decided you were going to write a play, I poked
fun at you, and heckled, and behaved in general like an all-
round grade-A crumb. You said I hijacked your self-respect
and you were right; that's exactly what I did. For that I
most humbly beg your forgiveness. (ANGELA *eyes him coldly*)
You asked me to take a look at things in New Haven and
Boston. I refused. Again I was wrong. I belong on your
team. I think my objectivity could have survived the added
strain . . .

DION Boy oh boy . . .

CHARLOTTE Shut up, Dion. Go on, Parker.

PARKER I don't know what happened in Boston, but I do
know this; if I'd been on your team, *nothing* would have
happened. So if anything *did,* then for my share of the
responsibility, Angie, again I most humbly beg your forgiveness.

DION Of all the presumptu-   IVY What is this; Backwards
ous, conceited, egotistical   Day??
. . .

CHARLOTTE   If the *two* of you don't shut up, I'm going to bang your heads together!

ANGELA   Parker—

PARKER   End of apologies. Now comes the unpleasantness.

CHARLOTTE   Parker, I don't think it's necessary to go into—

PARKER   Shut up, Charlie. Angie, I cannot and will not apologize for writing that review, nor for one syllable or semicolon in it. To my mind, which is the only measuring instrument I possess, *A Houseful of Silence* is exactly the monster I said it was. I've done my job, my readers have been warned. I know I take my work too seriously. Maybe it's because I feel that without their work people are vegetables. I may have heckled you and discouraged you, because I assumed that you had chosen the wrong work to be doing, *but I never tried to lock you out of your workroom.* Tonight you tried to lock me out of mine. (*Now* ANGELA's *ice is cracking again*) I want you to stay, Angie. If you try another play I won't throw spitballs. If you ask for my help I'll give it, because helping you when you ask for help is also my work; that dawned on me somewhere in the course of this evening; about thirty seconds ago, to tell the truth. But if you ever hint that I should write a soft review for you, or ask me to quit my job for one evening because you've chosen a job that happens to conflict with it, if you ever again say, "Hand over those tickets," so help me Hannah, I will knock out your two front teeth. That is what the poet meant when he said, "I could not love thee, dear, so much, loved I not honor more." (ANGELA *is liquefying rapidly*) Will you stay?

DION Tell me, would she retain the right to vote?

PARKER Yes, she would retain the right to vote. She'd retain all her rights except the right to step on my rights. Nobody has that. Stay, Angie. I love you and I need you. And John loves you and needs you too. Don't you, John? (*Louder*) I said "Don't you, John?"
   (*A beat.* JOHN, *in pajamas, steps sheepishly onto the landing*)

JOHN Yes. Please stay, Angie.
   (ANGELA *is all but melted*)

DION When do you bring on the violins?

PARKER (*Smiling at* ANGELA) I would bring on the New York Philharmonic if I thought it would help.

IVY Oh, Parker, damn you, why didn't you make that speech to *me,* four years ago?
   (*An awkward pause*)

CHARLOTTE Because you would have stayed, that's why.

PARKER Charlie . . .
   (*He looks with concern at* IVY)

CHARLOTTE I said it and I'm glad I said it . . .
   (ANGELA *wipes a tear from her cheek*)

PARKER Angie . . . Please . . . ?
   (ANGELA *looks at him for a long moment, then turns slowly to* DION)

ANGELA Dion . . . I—I . . .
> (*A smiling gesture of helplessness.* PARKER *expels the breath he's been holding*)

DION (*Going to* ANGELA) I'm not going to let you do this! (*Taking her shoulders*) You'll sit here and darn his socks and—and weave rugs and have a dozen babies— You'll *never* write another play!

ANGELA I will if I want to . . . I can do anything if I want to. (*Turning toward* PARKER) Anything . . . !

DION (*Drawing her back*) Sure, he talks big about helping you, but wait till you get out that typewriter and then you'll see what kind of—

PARKER (*On "you'll see"; the voice of authority*) Dion. (DION *stops, releases* ANGELA. PARKER *takes a step forward*) This is your father image speaking. (*Points upstage*) Beat it. In thirty seconds we're going to have "Spank-the-Precocious-Children Hour."

DION I'm not through yet, Ballantine; not by a long shot. She won't give Champlain *her* list, but I've got a list of my own to give him; of the drinks I saw you take this evening, and the booze that's reeking from you now. You were *drunk* at that theatre, chum, and a drunken critic is a dead critic.
> (*A beat*)

ANGELA I'm the playwright. I was with him all evening and I didn't see him take a single drink.

CHARLOTTE Neither did I.

JOHN Neither did I.

IVY His breath is pure Lavoris. (*Moving resignedly to* DION) Come on, Dion. You have to learn to lose gracefully, otherwise there's no applause on your final exit. (DION *moves upstage surlily.* IVY *puts on her coat*) So long, Parker. It was nice sitting next to you again.

PARKER So long, Ivy.

CHARLOTTE Don't take any wooden musicals.

IVY Johnny-Love . . . (*She blows* JOHN *a kiss; he waves his hand minutely*) I have two words of advice for you, Angela. Beef Stroganoff.
> (*She takes* DION's *arm and they exit.* JOHN *rushes downstairs and hugs* ANGELA. CHARLOTTE *rises and crosses to the dining table*)

CHARLOTTE Is *that* what that was? *Beef Stroganoff?* (*She inspects the aluminum container incredulously*)

PARKER (*Pointing at* JOHN) You! Into bed.

JOHN Yes, sir! Good night, Angie!

ANGELA (*Kissing him*) Good night, darling!

JOHN (*Going to the stairs*) See you in the morning!

ANGELA In the morning!

JOHN (*Going up, waving to* PARKER *and* CHARLOTTE) Good night! Good night!

PARKER Good night, John!   CHARLOTTE Good night!
(JOHN *exits.* ANGELA *drops off her coat.* PARKER *and* AN-
GELA *look at each other, and move forward*)

CHARLOTTE (*Putting aside the container contemptuously*)
Stroganoff—huh! (*She gathers the dishes and silver and
exits into the kitchen*)

PARKER Hello.

ANGELA Hello. (*They embrace*) Oh, Park! He was right!
Dion, I mean; about the rugs and the babies. I feel so—so
capable all of a sudden! (*They kiss.* CHARLOTTE *enters,
watches them for a happy moment*)

CHARLOTTE The well-bred thing at this point would be to
leave the living room, don't you think?
(*Laughing,* PARKER *and* ANGELA *move to the stairs, and
start up.* PARKER *holds back*)

PARKER Go ahead, darling. I'll be with you in ten seconds.
There's one thing I *have* to do.

ANGELA Ten seconds . . . (*Climbs the remaining stairs,
turns*) Nine, eight, seven, six . . .
(*She backs into the bedroom.* PARKER *dashes down and
into study, gets the white file box, brings it into the
living room, puts it down, leafs hastily through a hand-
ful of its slips*)

CHARLOTTE What on earth—?

PARKER Ah! Here it is! (*He takes one slip, puts down the
remainder*)

110

CHARLOTTE What?

PARKER (*Going upstairs*) A note to leave on my pillow in the morning! For Angie!

CHARLOTTE Parker! (*He stops on the landing*) I'm an old woman and I've had a grueling evening. Don't tease me. What does it say?
(*A beat*)

PARKER (*Grins, reads*) "Warm, vibrant, and thoroughly satisfying from first to last. The most delightful conception of the entire season!"
(*He exits into the bedroom as*

The Curtain Falls

III